I WANT
TO STOP
SMOKING...
SO HELP
ME GOD!

I WANT TO STOP SMOKING... SO HELP ME GOD!

A CHRISTIAN BASED APPROACH
TO USE WHEN QUITTING

JUDY MURPHY SIMPSON

Printed in the United States of America
First Printing, 2005
Christian Connection Publishing

Second Printing 2013
Electronic Kindle Book 978-0-9890078-9-4
Paperback via Lightning Source 978-0-9890078-1-8

WARNINGS, PRECAUTIONS & DISCLAIMERS

George F. Will, editorial columnist for *Newsweek*, once wrote a tongue-in-cheek article about the absurdity of some disclaimers in today's world:

> "Do not eat this sled.
> For best results, do not apply this
> floor wax to your teeth.
> This antifreeze is not intended for
> pouring on your breakfast cereal."

Reading this book does not automatically guarantee anything.

Frivolous lawsuits by consumers cause manufacturers and writers to attempt to absolve themselves of any and all possible responsibility and liability for their information and products.

Having said that, I would like you to know that I have sincerely made every effort to be honest, realistic and Christian in the spirit and content of this book. Following the Christian principles in this book is intended to change or improve the direction, intensity and focus of you, the reader. This is by specific intent, following God's commands to let go of the old and embrace the new (Christian) ways of thinking and living. But, only you, with God's help, can change your habits and priorities.

If you are 100 percent satisfied to remain a smoker, actively resist change or have no interest in developing a closer relationship with God, this book will have marginal if any benefit.

Anyone who has a suggestion, problem or dissatisfaction with the book's content is encouraged to contact me at judy1simpson@aol.com.

For the Lord God will help me; therefore I will not be disgraced; therefore, I have set my face like a flint, and I know that I will not be ashamed.

Isaiah 50: 7, New King James Version.

TABLE OF CONTENTS

WARNINGS, PRECAUTIONS & DISCLAIMERS 5

PREFACE 13

ACKNOWLEDGMENTS.. 15

"DEAR SMOKER" 17

ARE YOU PLAYING THE "I'LL TRY TO QUIT" GAME?......................... 19

CHAPTER ONE: IN THE BEGINNING.. 21

GOALS 23

AFFIRMATIONS.. 23

PRAYER 23

THE CHRISTIAN CONNECTION 25

THOU SHALT HAVE NO OTHER GODS BEFORE ME 27

SMOKING: A COMPLEX PROBLEM 29

MAKING THE COMMITMENT TO QUIT 31

WHATEVER WORKS IS THE "BEST" WAY TO QUIT SMOKING 33

GUIDING PRINCIPLES FOR SMOKERS THINKING ABOUT QUITTING 35

HOW OLD WERE YOU WHEN YOU LIT YOUR FIRST CIGARETTE?........... 37

JOURNALING ACTIVITY: WHEN I FIRST BEGAN SMOKING................ 39

ACTIVITY: PREPARING A QUITTING PLAN.. 41

ACTIVITY: MAKING THE COMMITMENT TO QUIT............................. 43

ACTIVITY: VISUALIZATION.. 45

CHAPTER TWO: FREQUENTLY ASKED QUESTIONS..................... 47

GOALS 49

AFFIRMATIONS.. 49

PRAYER 49

THINKING ABOUT QUITTING MAKES ME WANT A CIGARETTE........... 51

SMOKERS WANT TO KNOW 53

"HEALTHY LIVING" SUGGESTIONS 55

WEIGHT CONTROL.. 57

MORE "HEALTHY LIVING" SUGGESTIONS 59

EXERCISE AND REST... 61

NICOTINE REPLACEMENT PRODUCTS 63

TEEN SMOKERS 65

CLOSET SMOKERS 67

MANAGING A SMOKING HABIT 69

NEVER TOO LATE TO QUIT 71

MORE HAPPY ENDINGS 73

HOW I QUIT 75

ACTIVITY: GETTING IN TOUCH WITH SMOKING "BLIND SPOTS" 77

ACTIVITY: QUICK FIXES LEAD TO LENGTHY RECOVERIES 79

CHAPTER THREE: COMPLEX QUITTING ISSUES.................................... **81**

GOALS 83

AFFIRMATIONS... 83

PRAYER 83

IS THERE A RECOVERY TIMETABLE? 85

CRISIS QUITTING 87

WHAT ABOUT OTHER TOBACCO USE? 89

SUGGESTIONS FOR SMOKING COUPLES/FRIENDS QUITTING

TOGETHER.. 91

BEING AROUND OTHER SMOKERS, AFTER YOU'VE QUIT....................... 93

DEPRESSION 95

ACTIVITY: CRISIS QUITTING CHECKLIST 97

ACTIVITY: QUITTING WITH ANOTHER SMOKER? QUESTIONS

TO ASK YOURSELF & YOUR POTENTIAL QUITTING BUDDY 99

CHAPTER FOUR: UNDERSTANDING THE ADDICTION **101**

GOALS 103

AFFIRMATIONS...103

PRAYER 103

HOW DO I INVOLVE GOD IN THE QUITTING PROCESS?.........................105

WHAT NEED DOES A CIGARETTE FILL?...107

SMOKING: IT'S A CHOICE 109

AWARENESS COMES BEFORE CHANGE 111

QUITTING: A PERCEIVED LOSS OF CONTROL 113

SELF-PITY 115

I'D WALK A MILE FOR A CAMEL 117

DEVELOPING A POSITIVE ATTITUDE...119

FOSTERING UNCONDITIONAL SELF-LOVE 121

BREAKING HABITS 123

THE POWER OF NICOTINE...125

STINKIN' THINKIN' 127

JOURNALING ACTIVITY: IDENTIFYING WHAT YOU REALLY
WANT WHEN YOU THINK ABOUT A CIGARETTE.........................129

ACTIVITY: CHANGING YOUR SMOKING-RELATED BEHAVIORS...........131

CHAPTER FIVE: PREPARING TO QUIT **133**

GOALS 135

AFFIRMATIONS..135

PRAYER 135

THE PRICE YOU PAY TO BE A SMOKER..137

REMEMBERING PAST FAILURES...139

LETTING GO OF PAST FAILURES..141

PUSHING FEAR AWAY 143

KEEPING AN OPEN MIND TO GOD'S MESSAGE 145

CHANGE: NOT EASY FOR MOST OF US.......................................147

BLAME VS. RESPONSIBILITY...149

ANGER 151

ACTIVITY: PUTTING A PRICE TAG ON SMOKING COSTS 153

ACTIVITY: SORTING OUT THE JUNK 155

CHAPTER SIX: YOUR FIRST MONTH AS A NONSMOKER **157**

GOALS 159

AFFIRMATIONS..159

PRAYER 159

WHEN THINGS FEEL TOTALLY "OUT OF WHACK" 161

COPING DURING A CRISIS..163

WHEN TEMPTATION COMES CALLING...165

WHEN TEMPTATION COMES TO STAY 167

INTERNAL AND EXTERNAL ENEMIES 169

GOD'S PROMISES TO YOU 171

WANTING SUCCESS – NOW!..173

LISTENING TO YOUR BODY 175

AND IT CAME TO PASS 177

STAYING FOCUSED 179

ACTIVITY: LOOK FOR OPPORTUNITIES TO LIGHTEN UP.................181

ACTIVITY: ELICIT THE SUPPORT YOU NEED 183

CHAPTER SEVEN: ISSUES DURING THE TRANSITIONAL PHASE 185

GOALS 187

AFFIRMATIONS...187

PRAYER 187

MEDITATION, PRAYER AND BIBLE READING.........................189

COPING...191

PERSEVERANCE 193

ISOLATION FOLLOWING CUTOFF 195

LONELINESS 197

REWARDS...199

MAINTAINING BALANCE IN YOUR LIFE 201

ACTIVITY: MAKING A GOD JAR 203

ACTIVITY: SPEAK KINDLY TO YOURSELF 205

CHAPTER EIGHT: REMAINING A NONSMOKER.......................207

GOAL...209

AFFIRMATIONS...209

PRAYER 209

MORE ON WORK AND PERSEVERANCE 211

CONFIDENCE VS. WORRY...213

LIVING THROUGH THE TRANSITION 215

THE DIFFERENCE BETWEEN SUCCESS AND FAILURE...............217

AN ATTITUDE OF GRATITUDE...219

A PUFF AWAY FROM A PACK A DAY 221

ACTIVITY: TALKING WITH GOD 223

ACTIVITY: INTEGRATING CHRISTIANITY WITH QUITTING..........225

**CHAPTER NINE: INFORMATION & SUGGESTIONS FOR
NONSMOKERS** **227**

GOALS 229

AFFIRMATIONS..229

PRAYER 229

IS THERE ANY WAY I (A NONSMOKER) CAN CONVINCE
A SMOKER TO QUIT?...231

SUGGESTIONS FOR NONSMOKERS..233

COPING, AS A NONSMOKER...235

ISSUES NONSMOKERS MAY HAVE NOT CONSIDERED.....................237

WHAT A NONSMOKER CAN DO TO BE SUPPORTIVE OF
A SMOKER WHO CHOOSES TO QUIT..239

SUGGESTIONS FOR HEALTH CARE PROFESSIONALS.......................241

ACTIVITY: HOW I CAN SUPPORT MY SMOKER...................................243

ACTIVITY: IF MY SMOKER SHOULD EVER THINK ABOUT QUITTING 245

EPILOGUE...247

ABOUT THE AUTHOR...249

RESOURCE SECTION 250

TABLE: CIGARETTE NICOTINE LEVELS...251

HELPFUL WEB SITES...252

BIBLE VERSES QUOTED..253

SUGGESTED READING LIST 258

This is what the Lord says: "Stand at the crossroads and look; ask for the ancient paths, ask where the good way is, and walk in it, and you will find rest for your souls."

Jeremiah 6: 16, New International Version

PREFACE

This book is written to offer hope to smokers that if they choose to quit and are willing to work and persevere, they CAN quit. If smokers decide to read but not act on the suggestions, the information is of little or no value. Without action, the best intentions and hopes won't change a smoker's status.

While wanting to quit is the most important step in the process, desire is only the first step. The mature smoker knows that there will be glitches and speed bumps during the quitting process. Success in any goal or achievement starts with a decision, backed up by work and perseverance. This is certainly true when a smoker quits.

The decision to smoke or not smoke is a choice that each individual must make. If a smoker chooses to remain a smoker – regardless of the reason – that decision must be accepted. I feel a genuine sense of sadness for those smokers who choose to remain smokers, but I respect that it is their decision to make.

A number of themes are repeated throughout this book, including these:
All of life's challenges are more manageable when God is actively involved in the process.
Quitting is not easy.
Success requires work.
Perseverance pays off.

At the end of each chapter, suggested activities are listed. The goal is to break down the smoking habit by changing behaviors and attitudes connected with smoking. It is recommended that you do the activities, even if they seem irrelevant or boring.

Journaling topics are included because I believe that the process of recording thoughts, hopes and goals validates them and provides you with a written record of where you've been and where you're heading.

Earth and sky, hear my words, listen closely to what I say. My teaching will fall like drops of rain and form on the earth like dew. My words will fall like showers on young plants, like gentle rain on tender grass. I will praise the name of the Lord, and his people will tell of his greatness.

Deuteronomy 32: 2-3, The Good News Bible

ACKNOWLEDGMENTS

My faith in God and acceptance of His love, inspiration and the gift of salvation define who I am and what I most value. The Holy Spirit has inspired and guided me through all aspects of my life, including the writing of this book. Thanks and praise be to God.

So, it is with love and gratitude that I dedicate I WANT TO STOP SMOKING ... SO HELP ME GOD! to the glory of God. I would also like to thank the following:

My husband, Gordon (Cork) Platts, for his love, counsel, sense of humor and generous encouragement.

My mother, Frances Brown, for the sacrifices she has made, the love she has demonstrated and the tears she has shed.

My sons, Guy and Andrew; my stepson, Doug; my daughters-in-law, Jenny, Saori and Liz; and my grandchildren, Kristin, Tom and Julia, all of whom become more precious, appreciated and treasured with each passing day.

Special people in my life whom I love and who continue to smoke.

Family and friends who urged me to write this book and who provided motivation throughout the editing, writing and marketing phases.

Dan Poynter and his staff at Para Publishing, for his invaluable book publishing seminar.

Those who critiqued sections of my book: Nancy Akin, Marjorie Eisenberg, Anita Gordon, Greg Howland, Susan Howland, Don Hufhines, Mike Kubasak, Rev. Jack Lundeen, Shirley Lundeen, Leslye Lyon, Rev. Synde Manion, Jane Meyer, Cork Platts, Neva Porte, Gabriel Rivera, Jr., D.D.S., Rev. Stephen Weissman and Father Ed Wrobleski, whose suggestions and comments are greatly appreciated.

My book shepherd, Gail M. Kearns (To Press and Beyond, Santa Barbara, California), for her outstanding editorial skills and sage counsel. I am grateful for her many talents, including expertise in production, printing and coordination of all the processes.

Do not be afraid – I am with you! I am your God – let nothing terrify you! I will make you strong and help you; I will protect you and save you.

Isaiah 41: 10, The Good News Bible

Dear Smoker,

This book is written with one goal in mind: to give you accurate and helpful information about how to quit. I have been where you are now.

As a former, long-term smoker, I am aware of the difficulties involved in stopping smoking. I did not quit easily. I was whiny, grumpy and cynical – anything but positive. My fear of failure and my strong physical addiction to nicotine prevented me from believing that I could ever stop smoking.

But, by the grace of God, I did quit and eventually began a new career in the field of smoking cessation, working as instructor, counselor and staff trainer. I have personally witnessed the successes of thousands of smokers.

This book, by specific intent, is not a medical guide, since I have no medical training or education. I encourage smokers to contact physicians, pharmacists or dentists for medical conditions or questions. I also intentionally omit information that I believe most smokers already know, as well as information that does not seem vital to a smoker's success.

The process of quitting smoking is not easy, but the road to recovery has a happier ending. I urge every smoker to make the commitment. The rewards are worth every bit of the effort.

Sincerely,

Judy Murphy Simpson

Put into practice what you learned and received from me, both from my words and my actions. And the God who gives us peace will be with you.

Philippians 4: 9, The Good News Bible

ARE YOU PLAYING THE
"I'LL TRY TO QUIT" GAME?

❖❖

Smokers who have no intention of quitting often announce, "I'm trying to quit." This response is usually meant to placate non-smokers who may have been pressuring the smoker. By saying "I'll try to quit" the smoker hopes to avoid confrontation and get himself or herself off the hook.

On the other hand a smoker genuinely committed to quitting, will do whatever it takes to be successful. No ifs, ands or buts.

To illustrate my point, I will share a story about my son, Andrew. A few years ago he was preparing to fly to Japan. It would be his first meeting with the family of the woman he hoped to marry. Less than a week before his scheduled flight, I received a desperate e-mail from him: "How do you eat with chopsticks? Immediate instructions needed!"

"Practice. It takes lots and lots of practice," I advised. "If you begin practicing immediately, you'll get more food in your mouth than on your shirt before your first dinner with Saori's family."

The same principle applies when you quit smoking. It takes commitment to a goal plus practice. Lots and lots of practice. While I hope that you will learn a lot of things by reading this book, you must apply the information read. If you do, in time (about six weeks), your new habit of not smoking will begin to feel a normal and natural part of your life.

Now is the time to ask yourself, "Am I serious about quitting or am I playing games?" If you are serious, you won't try to quit. You will quit. With this book you have a plan, the tools and I hope the motivation to quit, once and for all.

The Lord who delivered me from the paw of the lion and from the paw of the bear, He will deliver me from the paw of the Philistines.

I Samuel 17:37, New King James Version

CHAPTER ONE: IN THE BEGINNING

❖

GOALS, AFFIRMATIONS & PRAYER

THE CHRISTIAN CONNECTION

THOU SHALT HAVE NO OTHER GODS BEFORE ME

SMOKING: A COMPLEX PROBLEM

MAKING THE COMMITMENT TO QUIT

WHATEVER WORKS IS THE "BEST" WAY TO QUIT SMOKING

GUIDING PRINCIPLES FOR SMOKERS THINKING
ABOUT QUITTING

HOW OLD WERE YOU WHEN YOU LIT YOUR FIRST CIGARETTE?

JOURNALING ACTIVITY: WHEN I FIRST BEGAN SMOKING

ACTIVITY: PREPARING A QUITTING PLAN

ACTIVITY: MAKING THE COMMITMENT TO QUIT

ACTIVITY: VISUALIZATION

"Harken to me, you who pursue deliverance, you who seek the Lord; look to the rock from which you were hewn, and to the quarry from which you were digged."

Isaiah 51:1, Revised Standard Version

GOALS

To integrate God into the quitting process.
To address smokers' issues as they consider quitting.
To introduce book themes and principles.
To consider new attitudes toward smoking and quitting.
To think about the impact smoking has had in your life.

AFFIRMATIONS

God has always loved me unconditionally and always will.
I let go of untrue beliefs about cigarettes and open my body, soul and mind to positive changes in my life.
I am no longer the same person I was when I began smoking.

PRAYER

Lord, You and You alone are the God I praise, thank and worship. With Your love and power, I can address and overcome any problem or temptation. I can also change my attitudes and habits to better reflect Your presence in my life. Please be near me, Heavenly Father, during the challenging and frightening days ahead. When I feel weak or alone, remind me that You are always with me. In Your Precious name I pray. Amen

Trust in the Lord always, because the Lord, the Lord alone, is an ever-lasting rock.

Isaiah 26: 4, God's Word

THE CHRISTIAN CONNECTION

The most important relationship that I have ever had or will ever have is with God. Yet for more than twenty years, I smoked before, during and after almost everything. I turned to cigarettes instead of to God.:

- When I needed wisdom
- To unwind
- When I was bored
- When I was angry
- To celebrate

Four years after I quit smoking, I felt called to work in the smoking cessation field. Ultimately I worked for three different companies, each of which provided me with excellent opportunities to counsel smokers and to learn more about what helps smokers quit and what doesn't.

One frustration that I experienced when working with smokers was my inability to mention God, prayer or Christian principles. While I followed each company's guidelines and realized why it was not acceptable for me to share my spiritual beliefs while counseling clients, I nevertheless felt disconnected from my faith.

But the Holy Spirit, my constant companion, planted a seed: "Some day, when you no longer have corporate constraints, you will write a Christian-based book for smokers who want to quit but don't know how."

My goal is to integrate my first-hand knowledge of what it's like to be a long-term, heavy smoker, with my training as a counselor, my teaching background and my Christian faith. But, be advised that being a Christian and reading a Christian-based book doesn't mean that stopping smoking will necessarily be easier or that you will have fewer challenges than non-believers. It does mean that you have the universe's most awesome power source with you.

There is a "God-sized" hole in every person that demands to be filled – by something that cigarettes cannot fill. Journal about your relationship with God and your relationship with your cigarettes as you read this book.

Moses speaks saying, "Do not make for yourselves an idol in the form of anything the Lord your God has forbidden. For the Lord your God is a consuming fire, a jealous God."

Deuteronomy 4: 23-24, The Good News Bible

THOU SHALT HAVE NO OTHER GODS BEFORE ME

God gave Moses the Ten Commandments so that the Israelites would know the rules – their duties toward God and their fellow men. God began speaking to Moses by confirming, "I am the Lord your God ... you shall have no other gods before me."

God expressly forbade the worshiping of any kind of idol, either literally or conceptually.

An idol is defined as a thing devotedly or excessively admired. Idols do not have to be in the traditional human or animal shape, like the golden calf that the Israelites worshiped in Moses' absence.

Think about how you value your cigarettes and the sacrifices you make every day to remain a smoker. Might God consider cigarettes to be your idol rather than Him? Ask yourself these questions:

- What is it that I must have in order to feel complete?
- To whom do I turn for strength and comfort during difficult moments?
- What is it that I can't be happy without?
- Do I rely on prayer or my cigarettes, at least a hundred times every single week?

If you live to have a cigarette, could it be that God is jealous? The Bible says that He wants to be the only God to whom His people turn for comfort, strength, inspiration and joy. Does your cigarette drown out God, who says, "Turn to me when you are afraid or lonely"?

God knows that His children like easy answers and quick solutions. That is why He specifically forbids idols and the worshipping of any other "god". He knows that we humans are impulse-driven and often do not use good judgment. God, and only God, is omniscient (all-knowing), omnipotent (all-powerful) and omnipresent (present everywhere). The cigarette is none of the above.

Consider that when you say "Yes" to cigarettes, you might be saying "No" to God.

He (God) is trying to teach us letter by letter, line by line, lesson by lesson. He offered rest and comfort to all of you, but you refused to listen to him. That is why the Lord is going to teach you letter by letter, line by line, lesson by lesson.

Isaiah 28: 10, 12-13, Today's English Version

SMOKING: A COMPLEX PROBLEM

Smoking is one of those bad habits that generates a long list of "I shoulds":

- I should quit.
- I should admit the harm that cigarettes are doing to my body.
- I should talk with my doctor about nicotine patches, Zyban or other prescription products proven to help smokers quit.

Intellectually, most smokers know that quitting is a worthwhile goal. But, at an emotional level, many smokers fear that they do not have the courage, perseverance or whatever it takes to quit.

One of the reasons smokers have repeatedly tried and failed is that they have not understood the complexity of their smoking habit. Veteran smokers have forgotten that learning how to smoke is a step-by-step process. It took months to become an experienced and addicted smoker.

Learning how to quit also takes time and is a step-by-step process.

Think of the smoking habit as similar to a large connected spider web, with hundreds of individual" threads". Think about disconnecting the smoking habit, one thread at a time. Yes, cutting through the threads, one at a time, would involve time and attention to detail, but eventually the web is destroyed.

The same principles and end result are true with smoking.

If any of you lacks wisdom, he should pray to God, who will give it to him; because God gives generously and graciously to all.

James 1: 5, The Good News Bible

MAKING THE COMMITMENT TO QUIT

Smokers are not ready to quit until they are ready to quit. It's that simple. It's that complex. Only you can decide if cigarettes belong in your past or if they remain in your present and future.

For many smokers a constant inner struggle goes on, as they think about whether to smoke or quit, for they agree with many, if not all, of the following statements:

- Smoking is harmful.
- Cigarettes and smoking-related expenses are costly.
- Most nonsmokers dislike smoking and do not want to be around smokers.
- Millions of people who once smoked have quit.
- Millions of current smokers want to quit.

Smoking probably feels like a heavy burden – like a heavy weight that won't go away. It is one of the high prices you pay every day for continuing the habit. But, unhappiness about smoking opens the door to change. You have the right, at any time, to reevaluate what is important to you and what you could change.

Yes, it is difficult to quit. But, it is also difficult to remain a smoker. Do you choose to deal with the challenges of quitting or with the consequences of smoking?

Deciding whether or not to quit is an intensely private decision. For many smokers, the most difficult part of quitting is making the decision. If you could be certain of success, how hard would you work? How motivated would you be?

Our great desire is that each of you keeps up your eagerness to the end, so that the things you hope for will come true. We do not want you to become lazy, but to be like those who believe and are patient and so receive what God has promised.

Hebrews 6: 11-12, The Good News Bible

WHATEVER WORKS IS THE "BEST" WAY TO QUIT SMOKING

❖

In my opinion there is no one "best" way to quit smoking. Any assistance, technique, person, program, product or combination thereof that successfully helps a smoker's effort is worthy of praise and congratulations.

Each smoker has a number of possible techniques or aids that might be helpful to use when quitting. Whatever convinces a smoker to quit or provides assistance during the quitting process is powerful, regardless of what anyone says.

The "Cold Turkey" approach is still the most popular way to quit. It leaves all the details, timing and coping techniques in the hands of each individual smoker. But, there are many smokers, like myself, who tried cold turkey and repeatedly failed. I suspect that I'd still be a smoker today if I hadn't enrolled in a quality smoking cessation program when I did.

There are many stop smoking programs for either group or individual use. This book is a perfect complement to any program you might choose to use. Think about what establishes credibility and confidence in your mind. Ask about the program's success rate and the instructor's qualifications.

What about hypnotists, nutritionists, herbalists and acupuncturists? I believe that some individuals working in those areas can help smokers have a healthier or more positive attitude during the quitting process. But my opinion is that these techniques and approaches, used without an integrated program, are of questionable value. Nevertheless, I encourage smokers to discuss their stop smoking goals with any practitioners they have confidence in.

My words of caution: be discriminating and selective. There are a lot of "Snake Oil Sams" out there. Run from any product, service or individual that promises quick fixes, with no effort required on your part.

Teach me your ways, O Lord: make them known to me. Teach me to live according to Your truth, for You are my God, who saves me. I always trust in You.

Psalm 25: 4-5, The Good News Bible

GUIDING PRINCIPLES FOR SMOKERS
THINKING ABOUT QUITTING

If you define smoking as a problem, quitting can be a goal to set. Once a goal is set, you can visualize, and then achieve success.

Do you remember the story I told about my son wanting to learn how to use chopsticks? (Page nine) His goal was to look as natural eating with chopsticks as he did with a knife and fork. My advice to him was practice, practice, practice.

No one is born knowing how to use chopsticks or a fork. Those techniques are learned and perfected through repetition. The same principles apply to changing any behavior pattern.

Just as my son probably wondered if he would ever become proficient eating with chopsticks, long-term smokers often feel overwhelmed at the thought of never having another cigarette.

So where do smokers thinking about quitting begin? Start by telling yourself that, "With God's help and my long-term commitment to success, I can quit." By steadfastly following these steps, you will stop smoking.

Guiding Principles To Follow
* Have faith in God and yourself.
* Acknowledge that smoking is a choice you face every day.
* Accept the truth about cigarettes and the power they have in your life. Embrace God's love and integrate it into the quitting process.
* Work hard.
* Don't give up.

Many of the core themes in this book, including the Guiding Principles, are repeated and reinforced in this book, to emphasize or expand on their importance during the quitting process, as well as throughout life.

Avoid the passions of youth and strive for righteousness, faith, love and peace.

2 Timothy 2: 22, The Good News Bible

HOW OLD WERE YOU WHEN YOU LIT YOUR FIRST CIGARETTE?

Most smokers started smoking as teenagers or preteens. One of the reasons is that youth are inherently rebellious. Tell a teen to not smoke and guess what? Then, there is peer pressure and group bonding that forms among young smokers. To be one of the guys or one of the gals, many teens believe that they must light up or be left out.

I encourage long-time smokers to think about the many ways in which they have matured and changed since smoking that first cigarette. Your values, goals and priorities are probably very different now than they were "back then". Most adult smokers have let go of other youthful fads and immature ways of thinking and behaving.

Crew cuts, long sideburns, bell-bottomed jeans and Beetle fan clubs may be part of your past but probably are not part of your current priorities.

The reasons why you smoke today are probably very different from why you began smoking so many years ago. Today, you may have a love-hate relationship with cigarettes. The habit continues not because you love cigarettes but because you don't know how to comfortably quit.

Now may be the perfect time for you to rethink your priorities and goals. If you are willing to go back to the beginning of your smoking days, and honestly examine these issues, you may be ready to let go of cigarettes.

Record your thoughts in a journal.

Do not conform yourselves to the standards of this world, but let God transform you inwardly by a complete change of your mind. Then you will be able to know the will of God – what is pleasing to him and is perfect.

Romans 12: 2, The Good News Bible

JOURNALING ACTIVITY:
WHEN I FIRST BEGAN SMOKING

❖

When you think about your early smoking days, what comes to mind?

It is important for you to recall and write about your physical and emotional memories related to cigarettes. The following questions may help you journal about your past:

❖ What feelings did you experience before, during and after smoking?

❖ Did you smoke in a private or public setting – alone or with others?

❖ Was peer pressure a factor?

❖ Did you ever discuss your early smoking experiences with friends?

❖ What were the "payoffs" of smoking? Increased self-pride? Feeling more grown up or sophisticated? Getting more respect from friends? For the most part, were the early smoking days positive experiences?

❖ What were the drawbacks or negative aspects of early smoking experiences? Eyes that burned or watered? Coughing, gagging or feeling sick? Regrets, shame or guilt about smoking? Lying to or hiding information about smoking from parents or friends? For the most part, was smoking a negative experience?

Record your smoking memories and recollections, both positive and negative, in a notebook or journal. Then write about the influence that time, experience and maturity have had on you since you smoked that first cigarette.

Next, think about a child, grandchild or special young person in your life – who may now be considering smoking. What advice or information might you, as a person who smokes, give to a vulnerable and loved adolescent? Write it down.

Get rid of those foreign gods that you have, he demanded, and pledge your loyalty to the Lord.

Joshua 24: 23, The Good News Bible

ACTIVITY: PREPARING A QUITTING PLAN

I intentionally do not include a detailed stop smoking plan in this book. Each smoker is unique, and no one plan will be appropriate or helpful for every smoker. Instead I ask you to create your own blueprint, taking your special issues and challenges into account.

I encourage you to make a decision about whether you will quit smoking. For those making the commitment, spend some time preparing your personalized quitting plan, based on your unique lifestyle, schedule and personality.

For example, if you like classroom settings, contact your local hospital or your physician to see where and when a smoking cessation class is being held.

If you prefer to quit on your own, spend some time thinking about other times you may have quit.

- What aspects of the plan worked and what didn't?
- When were you the most vulnerable?
- Who or what situation caused you to pick up that first cigarette, after you had quit?

My recommendation is to allow four to six weeks to prepare your quitting plan. During that time finish reading this book and do any other needed research or preparatory work.

- Complete the activities detailed in every chapter.
- Journal.
- Prepare a well-thought-out plan for yourself.

My observation, after having worked with thousands of smokers, is that those smokers who try to rush through the quitting process without a specific plan have a much lower success rate than those who recognize that long-term success takes time and planning.

Commit to the Lord whatever you do, and your plans will succeed.

Proverbs 16: 3, New International Version

ACTIVITY: MAKING THE COMMITMENT TO QUIT

If you have decided to quit smoking, write the following sentence in a journal or notebook, then sign your name and the day you will stop smoking. Post your written commitment in a visible place as a reminder and as motivation.

I, _____, CHOOSE TO STOP

SMOKING ON _____, 2_____.

This time-dated statement is your personal commitment. Everything else in this book – all other information, suggestions and activities – are intended to help you achieve and maintain your stop smoking goal.

For nothing is impossible with God.

Luke 1: 37, New International Version

ACTIVITY: VISUALIZATION

Create the future you desire by seeing it in your mind's eye. Imagine the plot that represents the perfect ending: you as a happy, proud nonsmoker. Visualization helps turn your goal into a reality.

As you visualize yourself not smoking, imagine the joy of having renewed energy, radiant self-confidence and the respect of family, friends and colleagues.

Each time you "replay" your mental videotape, add new details that provide you with additional strategies, incentives and motivations for quitting. Your doubts and fears will diminish as you move toward fulfilling, in real life, the picture you created in your mind.

Hear my cry, O God; attend to my prayer. From the end of the earth I will cry to You. When my heart is overwhelmed, lead me to the rock that is higher than I. For you have been a shelter for me, a strong tower from the enemy. I will abide in Your tabernacle forever; I will trust in the shelter of Your wings.

Psalm 61: 1-4, The Good News Bible

CHAPTER TWO: FREQUENTLY ASKED QUESTIONS

❖❖

GOALS, AFFIRMATIONS & PRAYER

THINKING ABOUT QUITTING MAKES ME WANT A CIGARETTE

SMOKERS WANT TO KNOW

"HEALTHY LIVING" SUGGESTIONS

WEIGHT CONTROL

MORE "HEALTHY LIVING" SUGGESTIONS

EXERCISE AND REST

NICOTINE REPLACEMENT PRODUCTS

TEEN SMOKERS

CLOSET SMOKERS

MANAGING A SMOKING HABIT

NEVER TOO LATE TO QUIT

MORE HAPPY ENDINGS

HOW I QUIT

ACTIVITY: GETTING IN TOUCH WITH SMOKING "BLIND SPOTS"

ACTIVITY: QUICK FIXES LEAD TO LENGTHY RECOVERIES

The end of something is better than its beginning.

Ecclesiastes 7: 8, The Good News Bible

GOALS

To address smokers' concerns, through accurate information.
To understand that quitting is complex.

AFFIRMATIONS

God is with me every step of the way.
I am a strong, confident person, capable of accepting and overcoming any and all of the challenges presented during the quitting process.

PRAYER

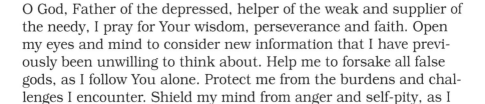

O God, Father of the depressed, helper of the weak and supplier of the needy, I pray for Your wisdom, perseverance and faith. Open my eyes and mind to consider new information that I have previously been unwilling to think about. Help me to forsake all false gods, as I follow You alone. Protect me from the burdens and challenges I encounter. Shield my mind from anger and self-pity, as I receive Your truth and peace. I ask these things through Christ, my Lord. Amen

This calls for endurance on the part of God's people, those who obey God's commandments and are faithful to Jesus.

Revelation 14: 12, The Good News Bible

THINKING ABOUT QUITTING
MAKES ME WANT A CIGARETTE

Smokers have many questions before, during and after cut-off day:
- Can I quit?
- How can I survive the quitting process and remain a non-smoker?
- How can I manage stress and anxiety without cigarettes?
- What about weight gain and mood swings?
- Are tranquilizers or patches a good idea?

Does it seem that everyone has an opinion, advice or a stop smoking story to share with you? Hopefully others' thoughts are genuinely motivated by love and concern for you, although much of what you hear about quitting is likely to be inaccurate.

For instance, I have heard people who quit more than twenty years ago say, "I miss cigarettes as much today as I did the day I quit, and you will too."

I find it hard to believe that statement. I doubt that many ex-smokers feel that way. Most former smokers are grateful and proud that they no longer smoke.

While you may be thinking about the hurdles, challenges and questions after you quit, balance those issues with a vision of your future benefits. How healthy and free will your life be without cigarettes? Remember:
- Good health is a worthwhile goal.
- Cigarettes contain poisonous materials.
- Your body deserves respect and protection.

I am the light of the world. Whoever follows me will have the light of life and will never walk in darkness.

John 8: 12, The Good News Bible

SMOKERS WANT TO KNOW

What Are My Odds Of Success?

There are no degrees of success. Either you quit or you don't. The final score is 100 percent or zero percent. There is no consolation in coming "close" to victory. It is the ultimate outcome that matters. There is no way to sugarcoat this reality.

What Are The Side Effects Of Quitting?

There are a number of side effects that may occur when you reduce your body's nicotine level. Three of the most common possible side effects are fatigue, thirst and "muddle-headedness" (feeling forgetful or unable to mentally focus as well as normal). Use common sense. If you feel:

- Fatigue? Get more rest.
- Thirsty? Drink lots of water.
- Muddleheaded? Maintain a sense of humor, and know that this feeling is temporary.

Possible emotional side effects include feelings of sadness, loss, anger or irritability. Any physical or emotional symptom that is extreme or long lasting should be discussed with a physician.

What About "Lite" Cigarettes?

If you believe that your smoking is "controlled" because your cigarettes are labeled "lite" or low nicotine, you may be among the most highly addicted. Smokers in this category use the words "just" and "only" to describe their brand of cigarettes or the quantity of cigarettes they smoke.

What Are The Most Common Causes Of A Smoker's Failure To Quit?

- Use of alcohol or drugs
- Unwillingness to persevere through challenges
- Anger
- Lack of patience – wanting a quick, effortless success
- Complacency after quitting – thinking it possible to have "just one" cigarette.

Therefore lift your drooping hands and strengthen your weak knees, and make straight paths for your feet, so that what is lame may not be put out of joint but rather healed.

Hebrews 12: 12-13, Revised Standard Version

"HEALTHY LIVING" SUGGESTIONS

In preparing to quit you may be concerned about weight gain, stress and related "healthy living" issues. I include some information about those subjects, and there is a wealth of data available from experts in those areas.

The few guidelines that I include in this book are common sense suggestions. But, having taught and counseled thousands of adult smokers, I know that many smokers during the quitting process do not demonstrate common sense. If you want to quit, I encourage you to practice these behaviors:

- Make time to stay in touch with the Lord, who seeks a close relationship with you and wants to be involved in your every day decisions, both large and small.

- Eat three small nutritious meals a day, with healthy, low calorie snacks in-between. It is important for you to eat something within the ninety minutes after rising in the morning.

- Drink lots of water. It helps to flush nicotine from your body.

- Limit sugar and caffeine intake, both of which provide you with a quick pick-up, then just as quickly reverse the effects.

- Limit or eliminate alcohol, for at least the first month after stopping. Alcohol can destroy your resolve.

- Get sufficient sleep. No one denied of sleep should expect to function effectively. The majority of people need seven to nine hours of sleep per evening. Eliminate unnecessary activities, if need be, to get sufficient rest.

- Exercise moderately, at least three times per week. Contact a physician before beginning a new or strenuous activity.

- Make time to laugh, relax, have fun and be loving to yourself and others.

Do you not know that your body is a temple of the Holy Spirit, who is in you, whom you have received from God? You are not your own.

I Corinthians 6: 19 - 20, New International Version

WEIGHT CONTROL

The fear of gaining weight is a major issue with many smokers considering quitting.

There is a correlation between smoking and metabolism. Nicotine constricts blood vessels, causing the heart to work harder. A smoker's blood pressure is generally (but not always) higher than a nonsmoker's would be. A smoker's metabolism is generally (but not always) higher than a nonsmoker's of the same age, weight, height and other significant variables.

Most research says that all other aspects being the same, a smoker gains an average of five to eight pounds during the year after stopping smoking. Few people welcome the thought of any weight gain.

If weight gain is a major concern, closely monitor your diet and increase your exercise activity by at least ten minutes a day. However, keep your primary focus on quitting smoking, not obsessing about a slight weight gain.

If after quitting you eat every time you think about a cigarette, you will undoubtedly gain weight. Do not make food a substitute for cigarettes. If you choose to substitute food to fill an emotional emptiness you cannot honestly blame quitting smoking for a weight gain. A more honest assessment of weight gain might be:

- After quitting, food tasted better, so I yielded to temptation and ate more.
- Every time I thought about a cigarette, I ate instead.
- I failed to demonstrate good judgment or restraint regarding when, what or how much I ate.

Remember, if cigarettes were the perfect weight control secret, there would be no overweight smokers.

Draw near to God and He will draw near to you.

James 4: 8, New King James Version

MORE "HEALTHY LIVING" SUGGESTIONS

❖

Deep Breathing

In her book, *365 Health and Happiness Boosters* M. J. Ryan talks about the value of belly breathing. She says, "When we are nervous, upset or anxious, we breathe only with the top part of our chest....

Belly breathing has been shown to reduce stress and anxiety symptoms by 63 percent. Take a long slow breath in through your nose, inhaling all the way into your abdomen. Feel it rise. Then slowly let your breath out all the way, imagining the tension leaving as the air does. As you exhale, let go of the tension in your face, neck and upper body. Relax your forehead, eyes, jaw and tongue. Be sure to breathe slowly through the nose; breathing through the mouth can cause hyperventilation and panic attacks.

Now all you have to do is remember to do it. Try putting a colored dot on your hand for the day. Every time you look down and see it, take a belly breath. You can do this anywhere – even in the heat of a tension-filled meeting!"

How Do I Best Handle Stress And Temptation?

Quitting smoking is a stress-filled experience.

Christ can be a powerful unifying force in your life, filling your heart with love and peace. When the gifts of the Holy Spirit are accepted, a believer feels mended, stitched together and held in loving strength and security. So, instead of feeling torn apart and exhausted, those seeking God's presence can pray for and receive the peace that passes all understanding.

Physical exercise has some value, but spiritual exercise is valuable in every way, because it promises life both for the present and for the future.

I Timothy 4: 8, The Good News Bible

EXERCISE AND REST

Let's be honest. Not too many people get excited at the prospect of exercising – especially someone who is quitting smoking. How much misery can one person handle?

There are plenty of benefits to exercising: metabolism is increased, enabling a person to burn off more calories; muscle tone is improved, which usually improves one's appearance; and most people who exercise regularly confirm feeling more energy and a positive attitude.

Of course, check with a physician before beginning any new exercise program.

After exercising, rest. The National Sleep Foundation says that 40 percent of Americans report feeling so sleepy during the day that it interferes with their activities. Fatigue makes a person irritable, reduces energy, impairs judgment and increases temptation.

Sleep deprivation raises stress hormones and is sometimes linked to hypertension and cardiovascular disease. One of the best ways to physically prepare your body to successfully stop smoking is to consistently get sufficient sleep.

Carol Kuykendall, a contributor to *Daily Guideposts* encourages us to remember the story of Elijah, who was tired and despondent after a hard day of defeating the Baal worshipers and fleeing from the dreaded Jezebel? "I've had it!" he told God. "I'm tired and I want to die." The Lord first let Elijah sleep peacefully under the juniper tree and then sent an angel to feed him. After rest and food, Elijah felt prepared to face his future and hear God.

Do not forsake your servants; come up to us quickly, save us and help us.

Joshua 10: 6, New King James Version

NICOTINE REPLACEMENT PRODUCTS

During the 1990's the nicotine patch became the highest revenue-generating pharmaceutical product ever sold. Millions of smokers, then and now, want to quit.

In addition to nicotine patches, Zyban, a prescription antidepressant drug, has been identified as an aid for quitting. It can be used alone or in combination with other nicotine replacement and nicotine delivery products, such as the nicotine patches, inhalers and lozenges.

Do these products "work"? Yes! My personal observation is that smokers using both patches and Zyban, in conjunction with a quality behavior support program and monitored by a physician, have the best opportunities for long-term success. When smokers feel better physically, by reducing or eliminating physical withdrawal symptoms, they are more successful and less vulnerable to depression, anxiety and nervousness.

What about nicotine gum? My opinion is that most people who buy it do one of three things:

1.) Try a piece or two, find the taste unpleasant and throw the rest away;
2.) Do not read or follow package directions and misuse the product, often getting an upset stomach;
3.) Become "hooked" on the gum and transfer nicotine addictions, from their cigarettes to the gum.

Always consult with a physician before using any prescription drug and follow all of the physician's directions. Under no circumstance should you use someone else's pills, patches or products without medical approval.

There are many individuals who are not good candidates for any nicotine replacement product, including persons who have certain medical problems or those who are taking other medications.

Also, anyone considering the use of a nicotine replacement product or delivery system should carefully read product information to be informed about potential risks or possible negative side effects.

Forgive the sins and errors of my youth.

Psalm 25: 7, The Good News Bible

TEEN SMOKERS

How should adults react to a teen's smoking habit?

That is a complex question for parents, teachers and concerned adults who realize that a teen or preteen is smoking. Their first reactions may be to punish, prohibit or preach. Regrettably, none of these actions is likely to convince a teen to quit smoking.

Youths will probably apologize and make whatever amends they feel will lighten their punishment. They will also be more careful about when, where and with whom they smoke. But will they decide that quitting is a good idea? Probably not.

Once a teenager has begun smoking (and inhaling) on a regular basis, the probability of a teen quitting is very low *unless* the teen is genuinely motivated to stop.

Many teenagers think they are invincible.
- If peer pressure was a factor in starting to smoke, and the teen has the same friends now, the buddies may actively or passively sabotage any quitting efforts.
- The adult motivations for quitting smoking, such as concerns about health care, aren't generally present among teens.
- Few teenagers are mature enough to see the big, long-term picture. Most of them can't imagine being thirty years old, much less being old enough to have tobacco-related illnesses or negative consequences.

Chapter 9 has additional information and suggestions for non-smokers.

You've set up your idols beside doors and doorposts. You've uncovered yourself to the idols. You've distanced yourself from me. When you cry for help, let your collection of idols save you. A wind will carry them all away. A breath will take them away. But whoever trusts me will possess the land and inherit my holy mountain.

Isaiah 57: 8, 13, God's Word

CLOSET SMOKERS

There are many closet smokers who go to extreme measures to hide their smoking habits. Some of these smokers resort to secrecy and deception because their employers prohibit smoking and/or refuse to hire or insure smokers. Other closet smokers live with or love nonsmokers who hold strong anti-smoking sentiments.

Rather than quitting, some smokers delude themselves into believing that hiding their habit keeps everybody happy. Instead, it is a means to postpone or perhaps avoid confrontation and accepting responsibility for their behavior.

To control their nicotine addiction without cigarettes, some closet smokers regularly use nicotine replacement products (usually gum or patches) or smokeless tobacco.

Regardless of the circumstances, closet smokers subject themselves to considerable pressure, spending much time and effort sneaking around. They are often people pleasers who are highly addicted physically and emotionally to their cigarettes.

Chapter 9 has additional information that may help nonsmokers better understand closet smokers.

Therefore, since we are surrounded by so great a cloud of witnesses, let us also lay aside every weight, and sin which clings so closely, and let us run with perseverance the race that is set before us, looking to Jesus the pioneer and perfector of our faith.

Hebrews 12: 1-2, Revised Standard Version

MANAGING A SMOKING HABIT

Some smokers who choose not to quit fantasize about successfully "managing" their smoking habit. They rationalize that if they could control when, where and how many cigarettes they smoked, they could have the best of both worlds: smoking but in a more acceptable way.

Such a smoker might think, "If I only smoked five cigarettes a day, it would be much less harmful to my body than what I'm currently smoking. Yet I wouldn't have to quit altogether. Whew!"

Like most fantasies this one rarely works. Few smokers are able to maintain a dramatically restricted pattern of smoking. Most soon revert back to their old smoking volume with the end result being that they chalk up yet another quit smoking defeat.

Rather than trying to manage your smoking habit, why not channel your energy into quitting?

But those who wait on the Lord shall renew their strength; they shall mount up with wings like eagles. They shall run and not be weary; they shall walk and not faint.

Isaiah 40: 31, New King James Version

NEVER TOO LATE TO QUIT

Sometimes I'm asked, "When a smoker reaches a certain age and has smoked for many years, hasn't the physical damage to the body already been done? Shouldn't you just accept that person's smoking habit and leave him or her alone?"

One of my favorite stop smoking success stories involved a woman named Joyce who lived in Oklahoma and had smoked for more than seventy years.

The initial call for help came to me from Joyce's middle-aged daughter. I learned that Joyce lived alone in a house with lots of shag carpeting. Because Joyce had very poor circulation in her fingers, she frequently dropped her cigarettes as she walked through her house. Then realizing that she had dropped a lit one, Joyce frantically searched the carpet for the burning cigarette.

Joyce's daughter was understandably concerned that her mother might burn down the house.

Much to my delight, and the surprise of everyone who knew her, Joyce did quit smoking. Even the stress of a tornado in a nearby town did not diminish her positive attitude or cause her to light up.

Joyce, who had never learned how to drive had kept her social outings to a minimum since none of her friends smoked. Once she quit, Joyce enthusiastically welcomed luncheon and shopping invitations.

There were many immediate benefits for Joyce:
The circulation in her fingers and toes dramatically improved within several months after she quit;
Her self-imposed isolation ended.

Joyce's daughter was very proud of her mother, although she observed, "When Mom was a smoker, I always knew where she was. Now that she's quit, she's never home It's quite a challenge getting in touch with her!"

Now that's a Happy Ending.

You will say in that day: "I will give thanks to thee, O Lord, for though thou wast angry with me, thy anger turned away, and thou didst comfort me.

Isaiah 12: 1, Revised Standard Version

MORE HAPPY ENDINGS

One of the most satisfying aspects of being a smoking cessation counselor is that I help empower smokers to dramatically improve their lives. It is an awesome blessing to witness the joy that quitting brings to a smoker and the smoker's family. I'd like to share two more "Happy Ending" stories with you as motivation and inspiration.

One of my clients, a closet smoker, was a college professor whose incentive to quit was that she would soon be expected to share a hotel room with one of her colleagues during an international professional conference. This brilliant woman had great self-confidence and success in every other aspect of her life.

But as her quit date approached, she discussed her doubts with me that she would be able to quit. Despite her work and preparation, she was afraid to visualize success. Instead her fear was that she would again repeat her past failures.

I am pleased to say that she did succeed. For years she sent me Christmas cards expressing her gratitude and excitement at being a nonsmoker.

I also remember a man from a Christian-based stop smoking class I taught in Santa Barbara, California. He had smoked for more than forty years. Using both nicotine patches and Zyban, which his physician had recommended, he later told me: "Not only have I quit smoking, which I never thought I could do, but my life-long depression is gone. I feel like I've climbed out of a deep, dark well and can finally see blue skies and sunshine. I am grateful to God and you."

I'd love to receive a letter from you, telling me of your success. You can make your hope to be a nonsmoker come true, and I sincerely hope that you do.

Beware lest there be among you or woman or family or tribe, whose heart turns away this day from the Lord our God to go and serve the gods of those nations; lest there be among you a root bearing poisonous and bitter fruit, one who, when he hears the words of this sworn covenant, blesses himself in his heart, saying, "I shall be safe, though I walk in the stubbornness of my heart."

Deuteronomy 29: 18-19, Revised Standard Version

HOW I QUIT

Several months after my husband, sons and I had moved into a larger home with a bigger mortgage payment, my boss threatened to fire me unless I participated in a smoking cessation program that the hospital in which I worked was sponsoring.

I was a heavy smoker – at least two packs of Pall Mall Gold a day –and did not receive the news well. Actually I was very angry but by the grace of God, the program I enrolled in (Smokenders) was excellent.

The instructor, Jan Sobel, said, "If you come to the meetings and do the assignments, you will stop smoking." I did not put any credence in her promise although I attended all of the classes and completed the assignments. Much to my surprise, I did quit, and you'd think I would have been pleased about that.

However, I confess that for the next six months I complained to everyone about everything. I was acting like a whiny kid – angry that the decision for me to quit had been made by somebody else. I embraced that anger for many months until finally the Holy Spirit screamed in my ear, "Get over it! The program worked, and you're better off without cigarettes."

Four years later the Holy Spirit made another powerful intervention, and I launched what would become a fifteen year career in the smoking cessation field. All of the resistance and anger I experienced have provided me with invaluable insights that I never would have understood had I not struggled with the addiction.

I am profoundly grateful that I no longer smoke and that God has allowed me to share my experiences with other smokers. May the Holy Spirit pay you a visit regarding your smoking habit.

As he (Jesus) walked along, two blind men started following him. "Have mercy on us, Son of David!" they shouted. When Jesus had gone indoors, the two blind men came to him, and he asked them, "Do you believe that I can heal you?" "Yes, sir!" they answered. Then Jesus touched their eyes and said, "Let it happen, then, just as you believe!"

Matthew 9: 27-30, Today's English Version

ACTIVITY: GETTING IN TOUCH
WITH SMOKING "BLIND SPOTS"

Bias is so easy to spot in others and difficult or impossible to identify in ourselves – thus the expression "blind spot".

All of us have our blind spots:
Things in our lives that we accept as true when in fact they are
false, and
Things in our lives that we reject as false when we later realize
they are true.

It is not easy for me to admit that I have been wrong. And the
more strongly I felt about something, the more difficult it is to
acknowledge an error in judgment, my own willfulness or my need
to be right.

Begin considering that you, too, may have some blind spots about
your smoking habit. You've probably heard the expression "smoke
screen" to describe something said or done to conceal or mislead
another.

Consider that the influence of your nicotine addiction, coupled
with the powerful manipulation of cigarette advertising, have
duped you.

Pray for an open mind, and the Holy Spirit will reveal your blind
spots to you.

My son, if you take my words to heart and treasure my commands within you, if you pay close attention to wisdom and let your mind reach for understanding, if indeed you call out for insight, if you ask aloud for understanding, if you search for wisdom as if it were money and hunt for it as if it were hidden treasure, then you will understand the fear of the Lord and you will find the knowledge of God. The Lord gives wisdom.

Proverbs 2: 1-6, God's Word

ACTIVITY: QUICK FIXES LEAD TO LENGTHY RECOVERIES

Historically, grocery stores stock "impulse products" (something you hadn't intended to buy) on the shelves adjacent to or attached to the checkout aisles. Everyone has to pay the cashier, and most of the time you have to wait in a line behind other shoppers and their carts.

As you're standing there, what else is there to do but look at the products around you?

Over the years I have seen all kinds of quick fix stop smoking products in the impulse product racks: tiny, pocket-sized books, magic filters, timers, nicotine gum and patches. I confess to having bought some of these products, wanting to believe in an effortless solution. Of course none of them worked.

Or maybe you have responded to a radio, television or print ad that promised immediate results for a stop smoking product or program.

What seems like a good deal rarely is. Not only did I not quit through a quick fix, each failure reconfirmed my belief that I would never be able to quit. So the quick fix products not only stole my money, they stole my hope for success as well as my self-confidence.

Resist the urge to try a quick fix.

But now thus says the Lord ... "Fear not, for I have redeemed you; I have called you by name, you are mine. When you pass through the waters I will be with you; and through the rivers, they shall not overwhelm you; when you walk through fire you shall not be burned, and the flame shall not consume you. For I am the Lord your God.

Isaiah 43: 1-3, Revised Standard Version

CHAPTER THREE: COMPLEX QUITTING ISSUES

❖

GOALS, AFFIRMATIONS & PRAYER

IS THERE A RECOVERY TIMETABLE?

CRISIS QUITTING

WHAT ABOUT OTHER TOBACCO USE?

SUGGESTIONS FOR SMOKING COUPLES/FRIENDS QUITTING TOGETHER

BEING AROUND SMOKERS, AFTER YOU'VE QUIT

DEPRESSION

ACTIVITY: CRISIS QUITTING CHECKLIST

ACTIVITY: QUITTING WITH ANOTHER SMOKER? QUESTIONS TO ASK YOURSELF AND YOUR POTENTIAL QUITTING BUDDY

Everything that happens in this world happens at the time God chooses.

Ecclesiastes 3: 1, The Good News Bible

GOALS

To understand that each smoking habit is unique.
To prepare for issues and challenges that may occur during the quitting process.
To accept that there are no "safe" tobacco products.

AFFIRMATIONS

Even if quitting involves unusual adaptations and adjustments, I can still succeed.
My desire to quit is stronger than any problems I may encounter.
If depression is a problem, I will contact my physician for help.

PRAYER

Gracious God, sometimes I look for excuses instead of solutions. I pray for an open mind that will enable me to accept and use new information about smoking and quitting. When I find myself resisting change, help me to feel Your presence and comfort as I face the fears I feel.

May I always remember that nothing is too difficult for You, and that with Your help, nothing will be too difficult for me either.
Amen

Blessed be the Lord your God, who has delighted in you.

I King 10: 9, Revised Standard Version

IS THERE A RECOVERY TIMETABLE?

God doesn't reveal all of life's details that lie ahead. Of course not. How (boring, exciting, sad, happy, challenging, fulfilling) would life be if you knew what tomorrow would bring? People read a book to find out the plot and the ending. In the same manner, you are to live life, one minute at a time, to find out what will happen in the future.

Yet, you may be wondering, **"When Will I:**

- Stop thinking about cigarettes?
- Feel "normal" again?
- Know that I'm "over the hump"?

It is impossible to predict a recovery timetable – either for a patient healing after surgery or for a smoker quitting. Each person progresses through the stages of discomfort and change in unique ways and timing. Those who are positive and follow a successful plan usually find the recovery process is easier.

Few of us enjoy change, yet change can provide a time and setting for incredible growth and faith building. Regrettably, it is usually only in retrospect that this truth is fully understood and appreciated. Consider accepting that wherever, whatever and whenever the stages of your recovery may be, you are in the exact perfect place.

Consciously work to let go of fear of the future. Christians don't have to know the answers to tomorrow's questions. "When" is a control issue. Only God has the wisdom and the ability to determine timing.

NOW is the only real time that anyone has. Living in the past can produce regret, guilt or despair. Trying to live in the future can produce anxiety, worry or fear. God can only share His love and strength with you now.

If you refuse to learn, you are hurting yourself. If you accept correction, you will become wiser.
Proverbs 15: 32, The Good News Bible

CRISIS QUITTING

People often make significant lifestyle changes when confronted with a crisis.

Fairly often, when smokers give reasons for wanting to quit, the response given is: "I have to quit." Often that person goes on to say that a doctor has warned or advised of serious health consequences if smoking is continued.

The truth, of course, is that even if serious health risks are involved, it is still a smoker's choice regarding whether or not to quit. In many addictions, people do not seek help until rock bottom has been reached or death appears imminent. Often that's true with smokers. Some smokers choose death over quitting. But, feeling up against the wall provides motivation for many smokers to quit.

My suggestions to smokers in the "crisis quitting" category would be to use the crisis as a launching pad, both to change and to renew faith in God. When everything in life is going well, it is tempting to take the credit for happiness. It is often during times of tragedy that many individuals finally realize that only God has true power and that with His help, they can demonstrate the desire and capacity for change.

There shall be no strange gods among you. You shall not bow down to a foreign god.

Psalm 81: 9, Revised Standard Version

WHAT ABOUT OTHER TOBACCO USE?

A large cigar is equivalent to four or five cigarettes in the amount of nicotine contained and has about twenty-five times as much carbon monoxide.

Snuff is a moist tobacco product made up of long strands of sliced-up tobacco leaves. It contains nicotine but not all of the toxins created when tobacco is burned.

Cigars, pipes, smokeless tobacco, snuff, "chew" and marijuana are not safe alternatives to cigarettes. There is significant medical research which shows that the regular or periodic use of any tobacco product is harmful to the user.

Medical experts agree that any form of tobacco use causes significant risk. Do not be deceived by tobacco manufacturer's slick advertising and marketing campaigns. All tobacco products are potentially deadly.

Each one should test his own actions. Then he can take pride in himself, without comparing himself to somebody else, for each one should carry his own load.

Galatians 6: 4-5, New International Version

SUGGESTIONS FOR SMOKING COUPLES/FRIENDS QUITTING TOGETHER

When a husband or wife or two friends decide to stop smoking together, it can be the best of decisions or the worst. It may strengthen or badly strain the relationship. It often happens that one person succeeds and the other fails.

In an ideal situation both individuals freely decide to quit, with each person demonstrating commitment, maturity and perseverance throughout the quitting process. But in reality, one of the quitters is usually more disciplined or handles the changes and challenges more easily.

The fact that two people love each other or are close friends has little to do with each individual's opportunity for success. Each smoker who decides to quit makes many choices that determine his or her final smoking outcome.

It is common for one quitter to play the role of the parent (you "should" quit), the judge (you aren't following the program) or the jury (you're going to be sorry if you cheat). Neither person is the guard or enforcer of rules, standards or achievements. As much as each person might like to ensure the mate's or friend's behavior, no one can carry another person to success. Let go of the thought that you can significantly influence, much less control another's outcome.

There is nothing that anyone can say or do that will "make" someone smoke a cigarette. There is nothing anyone can say or do that will prevent someone from smoking a cigarette, although one may blame the other if a slip or relapse occurs. If this happens, refuse to accept the offered manipulation or guilt. A smoker who successfully quits deserves "credit" for the success. Similarly, one who does not succeed must accept sole and complete responsibility for failing to quit.

Those who do quit sometimes feel sorry or even responsible for those who didn't. Yes, it is regrettable that not everyone chooses to remain a nonsmoker. However, no one needs to feel guilty for successfully quitting, even if the buddy didn't.

These are issues that should be discussed, in detail, before friends and couples set quit date(s).

Do not be fooled. Bad companions ruin good character.

I Corinthians 15: 33, The Good News Bible

BEING AROUND OTHER SMOKERS, AFTER YOU'VE QUIT

❖

Being around smokers after having recently quit puts you in a very vulnerable situation.

Some smokers who have no interest in changing their behavior may feel threatened or jealous by your decision to quit. Persons who smoke may try to talk, tease or manipulate you into lighting up. They may offer you a cigarette at a vulnerable time or appeal to your ego. Be aware. Be on guard!

For those who live or work with such a smoker, I suggest informing them about your decision to quit. Share this information several weeks before actually beginning the quitting process. This gives smokers some time to digest and hopefully accept your information in a mature fashion.

Ask your smoking friends to respect your decision to quit. After cutoff, ask smokers not to leave their cigarette packs lying around, in common shared areas.

Obviously, the rest of the world doesn't change just because you quit. Indeed, there may be other smokers in your close proximity. Acceptance of this and awareness of your vulnerabilities serve as preparation for how to best handle being around them.

Be aware of the times and situations that could be the most dangerous for you, including hunger and fatigue. To minimize these challenges, do not skip meals, and do not go more than five hours between meals. Get sufficient rest. Go to bed when you are tired.

Eliminate or greatly reduce alcohol intake for at least several months after quitting.

Much of this advice, which was given in an earlier passage, is common sense information but important enough to be repeated. Many smokers have a long history of poor eating, irresponsible drinking and inadequate sleeping habits. Not taking good care of your body makes you vulnerable to self-pity, despair, temptation and failure.

Forewarned is forearmed.

Behold, you are beautiful, my love; behold, you are beautiful!

Song of Solomon 4: 1, Revised Standard Version

DEPRESSION

Depression is a common problem. Smokers, especially those who are over the age of fifty, are particularly vulnerable to depression.

What is depression? General categories of depression could include:

- Occasional depression – what most people experiences now and then. It may or may not be related to a specific source or reason.

- Acute depression – a normal reaction to a specific cause.

- Chronic depression – occurs over a long period of time and can suck the joy from a person's life. What a person may feel is "swallowed up" or in a constant state of hopelessness.

It is estimated that 30-40 percent of adults who smoke suffer from depression. Research has shown that nicotine releases a surge of "feel-good" chemicals, such as beta-endorphins and dopamine. For this reason, smoking provides short-term relief for depression. Thus, for many, smoking becomes a form of self-medication.

Because even low levels of depression have been shown to dramatically affect smoking relapse rates, smokers with symptoms of or a history of depression are encouraged to discuss this issue with a physician prior to quitting smoking.

The vast majority of chronically depressed persons can be successfully treated with prescribed medication and can live improved, happier lives as nonsmokers. There should be no stigma, reluctance or embarrassment in asking a physician for help for depression or any other medical or emotional problem.

I do not claim that I have already succeeded or have already become perfect. I keep striving to win the prize for which Christ Jesus has already won me to himself.

Philippians 3: 12, The Good News Bible

ACTIVITY: CRISIS QUITTING CHECKLIST

❖

If you find yourself in a medical crisis, such as having heard the diagnosis of a serious illness or a physician's recommendation that major surgery is needed, your first thought may be, "There's no way that I could quit at a time like this!"

Your second thought might be, "Maybe there's no way that I will survive if I don't quit."

Regardless of your condition or the physician's orders, you – the smoker – are the only one who can make the decision regarding whether to smoke or quit.

❖ To help you sort out your priorities, ask yourself these questions:

❖ How much am I willing to sacrifice for my cigarettes? My life? An opportunity for the best possible medical outcome? Serious complications or compromising my overall health if I don't quit?

❖ Have I talked with my physician about my fear of not being able to quit?

❖ Have I asked about new medications, such as varenicline (which targets the specific mechanisms in the brain involved in nicotine addiction), with my physician or pharmacist?

❖ Is my physician willing to work with me if I choose to quit? If not, what other resource people might provide me with the guidance and motivation I need?

❖ Are there people in my life I can turn to for help?

❖ Are there solutions or resources I have not previously considered that might be appropriate now?

Do not try to work together as equals with unbelievers, for it cannot be done. How can right and wrong be partners? How can light and darkness live together? How can Christ and the Devil agree? What does a believer have in common with an unbeliever?

2 Corinthians 6: 14-15, The Good News Bible

ACTIVITY: QUITTING WITH ANOTHER SMOKER? QUESTIONS TO ASK YOURSELF AND YOUR POTENTIAL QUITTING BUDDY

❖

Before you make a commitment to quit with another smoker, there are some questions you need to ask yourself:

- ❖ Is my buddy a practicing Christian?

- ❖ Will I feel comfortable sharing my faith with my buddy and at the same time draw strength from his or her faith?

- ❖ Does it seem that we are equally committed to quitting?

- ❖ Have we worked together during other challenging situations?

- ❖ Is there a balanced give and take relationship or does one of us dominate the other?

- ❖ How will I feel if he or she is successful and I am not?

- ❖ How will he or she feel if I am successful and he or she isn't?

- ❖ Is the relationship with my buddy or the quitting outcome more important to me?

- ❖ What would be the best thing that could happen if we quit together?

- ❖ What could be the worst thing that might happen if we quit together?

Jesus said to those who believed in Him, "...You will know the truth, and the truth will set you free."

John 8: 31-32, The Good News Bible

CHAPTER FOUR: UNDERSTANDING THE ADDICTION

❖

GOALS, AFFIRMATIONS & PRAYER

HOW DO I INVOLVE GOD IN THE QUITTING PROCESS?

WHAT NEED DOES A CIGARETTE FILL?

SMOKING: IT'S A CHOICE

AWARENESS COMES BEFORE CHANGE

QUITTING: A PERCEIVED LOSS OF CONTROL

SELF-PITY

I'D WALK A MILE FOR A CAMEL

DEVELOPING A POSITIVE ATTITUDE

FOSTERING UNCONDITIONAL SELF-LOVE

BREAKING HABITS

THE POWER OF NICOTINE

STINKIN' THINKIN'

JOURNALING ACTIVITY: IDENTIFY WHAT YOU REALLY WANT WHEN YOU THINK ABOUT A CIGARETTE

ACTIVITY: CHANGING YOUR SMOKING-RELATED BEHAVIORS

I am in trouble, God – listen to my prayer! I am afraid of my enemies – save my life!

Psalm 64: 1, The Good News Bible

GOALS

To involve God in the decision-making process.
To reestablish hope, trust and belief in yourself, as someone who is capable of quitting smoking.
To learn from past mistakes, then to let go of anger and regrets.
To break the habit, one step at a time.

AFFIRMATIONS

God loves me just as I am, and I love me just as I am.
I can unconditionally love myself, yet still see my weaknesses, vulnerabilities and aspects of myself that I want to change.
Loving myself opens the door to a closer relationship with God and others.

PRAYER

Almighty God, source of all wisdom, You know my needs before I ask and my weaknesses before I confess them. Have compassion on me, I pray. Give me courage, O Lord, to make the commitment to quit smoking.

Open my eyes, mind and heart to visualize the rewards that I will realize in the future, rather than dwelling on negative feelings. Let me fear nothing because You are with me every step of the way. In Your name I pray. Amen

Your ears shall hear a word behind you, saying, "This is the way. Walk in it."

Isaiah 30: 21, New King James Version

HOW DO I INVOLVE GOD IN THE QUITTING PROCESS?

All of my family and friends know that I have worked in the smoking cessation field for many years, so they weren't surprised to learn that I was writing a book about quitting. They also know that I'm a Christian.

Yet when I tell people that I'm writing a Christian-based stop smoking book, a common question is, "What does quitting have to do with God?" What they are really asking is why I don't write a smoking cessation book that doesn't include any mention of God, the Bible or my Christian beliefs.

The answer is that I wouldn't dream of not including God in such an important decision and process.

The next question I usually receive is, "What about smokers who aren't Christians?" I respond that, while I would want any smoker desiring to quit success, I offer no apologies for the Bible verses or the Christian philosophy that I include.

If cigarettes are a problem in your life, and you are a Christian, I strongly encourage you to actively involve God in the quitting process by:
- Integrating your faith in all aspects of your life.
- Asking God for help.
- Opening your heart, mind and body to hear and receive His help.
- Following the directions the Holy Spirit gives you.
- Giving God thanks, praise and credit before you quit, as you quit and after you quit.

Expect that God hears your prayers. He does. Expect to receive His love and strength. You will. Expect powerful angels to be with you during challenges and struggles. They will.

The Ryder truck rental company's slogan is: "Together we are going places". That's the way I feel about God: as long as I embrace Him in everything I do and say, I will be able to manage whatever happens.

Could your new slogan be: Together God and I are going places, and I no longer need to take cigarettes?

An attacker advances against you ... guard the fortress, watch the road, brace yourselves, and marshal all your strength.

Nahum 2:1, New International Version

WHAT NEED DOES A CIGARETTE FILL?

It is not as important how many cigarettes you smoke per day as why and when you smoke. It is important for you to identify your smoking details. Ask yourself, "Is my cigarette:

- A little buddy?
- A way of dealing with my loneliness, rejection, low self-esteem, pain?
- A way to provide me with comfort or a reward?
- A way of acting out or rebelling against others?
- A security blanket – when I don't have anyone or anything else to turn to?
- A way to have privacy and isolation?"

By better understanding the many intricate and intertwining aspects of smoking and how they impact your life many times every day, you can begin letting go of your cigarettes – physically, mentally and emotionally.

These insights may also help you to identify why it has been so difficult for you to quit in the past, despite your desire and motivation. As the Holy Spirit reveals your blind spots to you, you will find it easier to break your ties to cigarettes.

I call heaven and earth as witnesses today against you that I have set before you life and death, blessing and cursing; therefore choose life that both you and your descendants may live.

Deuteronomy 30: 9, New King James Version

SMOKING: IT'S A CHOICE

The choice before you is to continue smoking or to quit. That choice is available to you many times every day, whether you consciously acknowledge the choice or not. Do you continue your addiction or do you end it? Do you worship the false god (nicotine) or do you reach out to God and forsake cigarettes?

You are not a victim. To the contrary: you are a child of God, capable at any time of being filled with His resolve and power. With faith you can visualize your future without cigarettes. Without faith all you have are memories of your past with cigarettes, daily challenges and embarrassments about being a smoker and your fears about a cigarette-less future.

Achieving dreams and goals always include choices – acceptance of the truth, the desire to change, making needed adjustments, letting go of some "stuff" and not giving up.

- Include God in all phases of the process.
- Set your stop smoking goal and quit date.
- Begin to change your old smoking-related habits.
- Persevere with your new habits that will prepare you to quit.

You may ask yourself, "How could I have a comfortable and happy life without cigarettes? That would be impossible to imagine!"

Consider that if cigarettes are the last things in life you would choose to let go of, cigarettes represent for you your real power source. A truth to remember is that God's power and rewards far surpass the temporary relief that cigarettes or anything else could ever provide.

Peace is what I leave with you; it is my own peace that I give you. I do not give it as the world does. Do not be worried and upset; do not be afraid.

John 14: 27, The Good News Bible

AWARENESS COMES BEFORE CHANGE

It is estimated that 80 percent of our emotions, feelings and drives are unconscious in nature. What a challenge: fighting what can't be seen, heard, smelled or touched.

As a smoker you should be aware that there is a great deal of hidden or unknown information about the power of nicotine, including your acceptance of cigarette manufacturers' manipulative messages and inaccurate propaganda.

Awareness comes before change. If you are willing to examine facts about smoking and nicotine addiction, as well as your personal relationship to cigarettes, then you have taken an essential step toward identifying and eventually ending your emotional connections to cigarettes.

Contrary to what cigarette manufacturers acknowledge in their advertising messages:
- Cigarette companies deliberately and skillfully direct their products to youth, knowing that mature adults are much less susceptible to their deceptive marketing strategies.
- Millions of smokers hate and resent the negative aspects of smoking, even as they continue to smoke.
- Smoking is a complex habit that is not easily ended. No single action, assignment, distraction or nicotine replacement product can magically or easily enable a smoker to quit.

Ask yourself, "Would I have been as likely to smoke if the Marlboro man was pictured as an old man dying of lung cancer or the Virginia Slims model was a chubby grandmother hooked up to an oxygen tank?"

If the movies, billboards and print ads had depicted smoking as something that only the old people and despicable and villains did, would lighting up have had such an appeal for you?

If you are a mature smoker, you now have knowledge, abilities and wisdom that you did not have when you lit your first cigarette. It is not too late to change any habit or thoughts about smoking and quitting that you choose.

Forgetting what is behind and straining toward what is ahead, I press on toward the goal to win the prize.

Philippians 3: 13-14, New International Version

QUITTING: A PERCEIVED LOSS OF CONTROL

One of the most challenging barriers for smokers to understand and overcome is the misconception that cigarettes give them more control in their lives.

Why do smokers believe that cigarettes help them maintain control? Because nicotine temporarily delivers a physical lift, a smoker feels better physically for a few minutes after lighting up. Gradually, after years of lighting up and feeling better each time that he or she did so, a smoker starts believing that cigarettes can make anything better. Smokers then begin to smoke whenever they need a fast acting "pick-up". It is at this point that the smoker is truly emotionally "hooked".

All of us have control issues. We want:
- Order and predictability.
- To make decisions of our own free will.
- To be respected and accepted, just as we are.
- To determine the details in our lives. Do I drink lemonade or iced tea?

For most of us there is a comfortable, familiar feeling when we settle into established habits and routines. That is one reason why the thought of quitting is so unsettling, for stopping smoking totally rearranges a smoker's life. Suddenly nothing is quite the same as before. Nothing feels "right". It may feel like there is no control or order in your life.

Have coffee without a cigarette? Get ready for work and not light up? Start the car ignition and not push in the cigarette lighter? Drive anywhere without smoking? Not have a reward to look forward to? Not have a cigarette when you are relaxing or celebrating? Unimaginable.

It is important for you to understand that nicotine is a powerful and very addictive drug that controls you. You have only limited ability to control the addiction. Yes, some smokers demonstrate enough self-control to space their cigarettes or the circumstances in which they smoke but, who or what is really in control? Is it the smoker or the addiction?

And the God of all grace, who called you to His eternal glory in Christ, after you have suffered a while, will Himself restore you and make you strong, firm and steadfast. To Him be the power forever and ever. Amen.

I Peter 5: 10 – 11, New King James Version

SELF-PITY

Smokers, contemplating quitting, are prone to self-pity. And whining. And manipulating. Some are very good at all three:

- Life isn't fair.
- Quitting is too hard.
- I can't give up my cigarettes.
- Can't I just cut back?
- What if I just smoked lites?
- Maybe I'll try to quit after the holidays.
- At this stage of my life, aren't I entitled to one enjoyment without feeling guilty?

An extension of a smoker's self-pitying behavior could include playing the "If Only" game.

- If only I hadn't smoked that first cigarette.
- If only I'd quit thirty years ago.
- If only my spouse didn't smoke.
- If only I didn't have so much stress in my life.

A smoker wallowing in self-pity does not assume responsibility for his or her smoking. Instead, a smoker may play the role of a helpless victim – unable to honestly look at life, able to respond to a crisis only by lighting a cigarette while blaming something or someone else.

By using their problems or stress as excuses for not quitting, some smokers attempt to justify why it is okay to continue smoking. Instead of choosing to quit, they choose to feel sorry for themselves.

Self-pity is like a stray cat. The more you feed it, the longer it will hang around and find its home with you.

Now this is what the Lord Almighty says, "Give careful thought to your ways."

Haggai 1: 5, New International Version

I'D WALK A MILE FOR A CAMEL

The writer of that slogan surely understood the power of nicotine addiction.

As smokers learn more about addiction – how physically, mentally, behaviorally and emotionally attached they are – they realize that they have unwittingly accepted a full carton of lies, misconceptions and outright manipulations that have been masterfully written and delivered by cigarette manufacturers.

For many cigarette smokers, the term "addiction" means being hooked on an illegal drug. They may think of addicts as being dependent on heroin or cocaine, not over-the-counter cigarettes.

Yet, a number of legal substances, including food, alcohol, prescription medications, over the counter drugs, and cigarettes, that provide short-time pleasure, also have the potential for abuse, dependency and life threatening negative consequences.

Few people would deliberately choose to become an addict. Fewer still could imagine a person saying that he or she enjoys being an addict. Yet millions of smokers believe that they smoke because they enjoy it.

Many smokers are so manipulated and controlled by the power of nicotine that they are unable or unwilling to admit the height, width and depth of their addiction. Are you one of those smokers?

I am the Lord who created you; from the time you were born, I have helped you. Do not be afraid.

Isaiah 44: 2, Today's English Version

DEVELOPING A POSITIVE ATTITUDE

How would you describe your attitude toward quitting? Have you given up hope, assuming that you will never succeed?

The Bible is filled with stories about people who were afraid to believe that they could complete God's assignments: Moses, Gideon, Jeremiah, Jonah and Paul, to name just a few.

Stopping smoking can be a faith-building experience for obedient Christians, even in the face of fear and uncertainty. How you feel about quitting, to a very large extent, determines your success or failure. A smoker who feels depressed or angry about quitting is literally self-sabotaging.

One of the first challenges you should address is eliminating hopeless thinking:

- This will never work. Nothing ever works.
- I've tried everything.
- I just can't do this.
- I've failed before, and I will fail this time too.

Worry and lack of faith are two of the biggest obstacles anyone ever faces. Instead, choose to claim God's promises. Believe that you can quit. Believe it with every ounce of your being. Exchange fear and anxiety for trust in God and trust in yourself.

People become what they believe. If you spend a great deal of time thinking about regrets and failures, of course you will feel negative much of the time. But an attitude can be changed. Yes! Anyone can become a more positive, successful person. Practice, practice, practice.

Visualize the success you want to have happen and call on the power of the Holy Spirit to make every thought obedient to Christ's will. The Lord Almighty says, "Not by power, not by might, but by My spirit."

Love your neighbor as yourself.

Romans 13: 9, New International Version

FOSTERING UNCONDITIONAL SELF-LOVE

Many smokers are ashamed or embarrassed to be smokers and may define themselves by their failure to quit. They are reminded every time they light a cigarette that they have failed, in one important measure of success.

Are you frequently criticized or ridiculed because you smoke? If so, is it any wonder that your self-esteem may feel bruised? When you think poorly of yourself, you are less likely to achieve your goals and are more likely to experience chronic problems, such as fatigue, boredom and a lack of confidence.

Those who are the most successful in breaking undesirable habits are those individuals who expect to get what they want and are willing to do whatever it takes.

As Norman Vincent Peale outlined in his book, *Stay Alive All Your Life*, a person can succeed at anything, if goals are set and these steps are followed:

* Decide that you are through being dominated by an inferiority complex.
* Start filling the mind with an affirmative faith in God.
* Believe humbly, but strongly, in yourself.
* Start living in the belief that God is with you, helping you.

The subject of God's unconditional love for everyone is one of the central themes in the Bible and in this book. No circumstance or challenge exceeds His power.

Put away the foreign gods that are among you, and purify yourselves and change your garments.

Genesis 35: 2, Revised Standard Version

BREAKING HABITS

Smoking becomes an automatic response after years of practice. I once estimated the number of cigarettes I had smoked. To do that I multiplied 40 cigarettes a day X 365 days a year X 22 years of smoking. Is it any wonder that having smoked an estimated 321,000 cigarettes, one of my biggest challenges as I prepared to quit was removing the thought of having a cigarette from my mind?

For smokers who have spent many years "perfecting" their smoking habit, doesn't it seem reasonable that it will take some time to unlearn it? Being patient and loving with yourself throughout the quitting process may be difficult for you to do.

You may feel overwhelmed by learning new skills or mastering what seems like an impossible goal. But, instead of seeing quitting as an impossibility, consider that any habit can be taken apart and separated into small, "bite-sized" parts, each of which is manageable.

One important message that smokers need to believe and regularly remind themselves of is: I learned how to smoke in a step-by-step process, over a period of time. I will learn how to quit in a step-by-step process, over a period of time.

As you continue complete each day's new behaviors, one change at a time, one day at a time, long-term success will follow.

The Lord Almighty, has this to say: "I am the first, the last, the only God; there is no other god but me."

Isaiah 44: 6, The Good News Bible

THE POWER OF NICOTINE

I have worked with a wide variety of smokers – from teenagers to those in their eighties. Their accomplishments and career paths range from quite modest to most impressive. I have counseled housewives and judges; some of my former clients were on welfare and some are listed in various *Who's Who* directories.

Regardless of how you might choose to label or identify any of these smokers, thousands of them have told me that they list their stop smoking success as one of the single greatest accomplishments they have ever achieved.

- More important than becoming the president or CEO of a company;
- More important than owning a $10 million house;
- More important than being identified as one of Hollywood's most beautiful women.

One former smoker shared his journal notes in which he said, "I once:

- Renounced all other power but the nicotine god.
- Gave all of my allegiance and commitment to my cigarettes.
- Lost the respect of my family and friends who clearly saw that the cigarette's influence exceeded theirs.
- Compromised my physical, mental, emotional and spiritual health and well-being, and perhaps those of others.

Consider that anyone who smokes may have also accomplished everything on that man's list.

The good news is that it's not too late for you to rewrite your life story. Your future can be very different from your past and your present. Write the happy ending you'd want as the last chapter of your smoking history.

Has the Lord as great a delight in burnt offerings and sacrifices, as in obeying the voice of the Lord? Behold, to obey is better than sacrifice ... for rebellion is as the sin of divination and stubbornness is as iniquity and idolatry.

I Samuel 15: 22-23, Revised Standard Version

STINKIN' THINKIN'

There is a tendency in many smokers to rebel against authority and rules. This trait may help explain why it is also common for smokers to rationalize why it is okay to follow only selected parts of a stop smoking program. That kind of logic falls into "stinkin' thinkin'" mentality.

Smokers who are serious about quitting will accept that ending an addiction means letting go of the denial and manipulation that are a core part of the smoking habit.

Some of the principles in *I WANT TO STOP SMOKING ... SO HELP ME GOD!* may seem unimportant, but each suggestion and behavior change has a purpose and is part of the Big Picture.

To illustrate the point, think about a jigsaw puzzle. Some puzzle pieces are exciting and obvious; others are b.o.r.i.n.g. Perhaps most of the pieces are the same color ... dozens and dozens of nearly identical pieces.

At the end of completing the 1,000-piece puzzle, 999 pieces may be in place. But what happens if one of those boring little pieces is missing? The puzzle remains incomplete and unfinished. The absence of that one little piece is quite noticeable at the end. The potentially perfect picture is flawed.

The same point can be made for smokers who think that they can cut corners and not have the final outcome affected. Some behavioral changes suggested in this book may not generate much excitement. They may seem unnecessary or too time-consuming. Someone reading this book may feel tempted to try the cafeteria approach: pick out what looks attractive and leave the rest.

Resist that temptation.

Let him not deceive himself by trusting what is worthless, for he will get nothing in return.

Job 15: 31, New International Version

JOURNALING ACTIVITY: IDENTIFYING WHAT YOU REALLY WANT WHEN YOU THINK ABOUT A CIGARETTE

❖

As a smoker you often didn't ask yourself why you were reaching for a cigarette. You just lit it and smoked it. Now you need to break that automatic response, so ask yourself: What situations trigger the thought of a cigarette?

- Before you go to work?
- Before you go to bed?
- Before, during or after a crisis?
- When you are with people you don't feel comfortable with?
- When you're bored or killing time?
- When making an important decision?
- When angry or insecure?
- When celebrating or relaxing?
- When feeling rejected or abandoned?
- After failure to achieve a goal, deadline or expectation?
- After achieving a goal, deadline or expectation?

As I've already admitted, I once smoked before, during and after almost everything.

Think about the role smoking plays in your daily life and acknowledge the power you have given to cigarettes. Write about what situations and emotions trigger the thought of a cigarette. Then, write what you could do instead of having a cigarette.

My dear friends, do not be surprised at the painful test you are suffering, as though something unusual were happening to you. Rather, be glad that you are sharing Christ's suffering, so that you may be full of joy when his glory is revealed.

I Peter 4: 12-13, The Good News Bible

ACTIVITY: CHANGING YOUR SMOKING-RELATED BEHAVIORS

WEEK ONE

Become aware of how and when you most crave cigarettes. Common smoking "triggers" include:

- With favorite beverages (coffee, soft drinks, alcohol);
- Before and after meals;
- When hungry, tired, lonely, angry, bored or stressed;
- When waiting and having time "to kill".

If you routinely have a cigarette when you feel hungry, angry, lonely, tired or bored, think of the power you have given to your cigarettes. As you identify your predictable smoking times and situations, you have the chance to reclaim your power back from cigarettes.

To start breaking your smoking patterns, gradually change the details of your routines that have included having a cigarette. For example, decide not to smoke while drinking coffee, soda or alcohol. By choosing to either smoke or to drink a favorite beverage, you will begin to break some of your behaviors connected to cigarettes.

Switch to a different brand of cigarettes, always to a lower nicotine level. (See Table: Nicotine Levels in the Resource Section of this book.) Do not smoke menthol cigarettes. (If smoking non-menthol feels difficult, gradually wean yourself off mental cigarettes.)

WEEK TWO

Continue all of week one activities.
Change to a "lite" cigarette. If you are already smoking a lite cigarette, switch to an ultralite. By doing so, you are further decreasing the amount of nicotine in your body.

WEEK THREE

Continue all of the previous weeks' activities.
Smoke only ultra lite cigarettes. (Now or Carlton, 1 mg. nicotine)
Choose to not smoke:
In your vehicle,
Before eating breakfast,
When talking on the phone.

Let the Spirit direct your lives, and you will not satisfy the desires of the human nature.

Galatians 5: 16, The Good News Bible

CHAPTER FIVE: PREPARING TO QUIT

GOALS, AFFIRMATIONS & PRAYER

THE PRICE YOU PAY TO BE A SMOKER

REMEMBERING PAST FAILURES

LETTING GO OF PAST FAILURES

PUSHING FEAR AWAY

KEEPING AN OPEN MIND TO GOD'S MESSAGE

CHANGE: NOT EASY FOR MOST OF US

BLAME VS. RESPONSIBILITY

ANGER

ACTIVITY: PUTTING A PRICE TAG ON SMOKING COSTS

ACTIVITY: SORTING OUT THE JUNK

Now may the God of hope fill you with all joy and peace in believing, that you may abound in hope by the power of the Holy Spirit.

Romans 15: 13, New King James Version

GOALS

To learn from past behaviors, yet let go of blame, doubt and fear.
To visualize, then achieve the desired changes and success.

AFFIRMATIONS

I will not define myself by yesterday's failures.
I will tap into my strengths and desire to stop smoking.

PRAYER

Loving Father, I pray that you will show me how to increase my confidence in You and in me. Your guidance and direction are needed as I plan to quit smoking. Help me to trust that You, who know all my weaknesses, fears and past failures, will guide, direct and strengthen me throughout the quitting process.

Prepare me for the temptations that I will face, whether they will come from other smokers, people I love or from as yet unknown sources. When I feel my resolve weakening or start questioning whether now is really a good time to quit, please make Your presence felt. And, dear God, I ask You to provide whatever else it is that I need.

In Your precious name I pray. Amen

Blessed is the man who trusts in the Lord, whose trust is the Lord.

Jeremiah 17: 7, Revised Standard Version

THE PRICE YOU PAY TO BE A SMOKER

Smokers preparing to quit tend to focus on feelings of loss – on what they might miss after quitting.

Instead consider focusing on what you will gain by quitting and the negative factors that you will eliminate, for smoking slows you down physically, mentally, emotionally and spiritually.

Physically - You may believe that your lowered energy level is re-lated to your age. Actually, fatigue and health problems are made worse by smoking. Indisputable medical research shows that imme-diate and long-lasting physical improvements occur when a smoker quits. The good news is that the human body works to repair itself.

Mentally - Many smokers do not think highly of themselves. Instead of acknowledging the areas in which they have been suc-cessful, smokers often experience shame, guilt or anger.

Emotionally - Smokers may use cigarettes to distract or distance themselves from addressing "uncomfortable" issues, such as per-sonal, family or work conflicts. Smoking is tied to avoiding emo-tions rather than talking about or working to resolve problems.

Spiritually - Christian smokers may feel embarrassed and out of place around nonsmoking Christians. This may limit their partici-pation in church activities or friendships with nonsmoking and/or Christian friends.

Cigarettes probably control many aspects of your life: your self-im-age, the friends you choose, where and with whom you spend time and the comfort level you feel in social and professional settings. Is your life governed by cigarette-related thoughts, such as:
- How long will the (movie, play or ballgame) last?
- Where is smoking permitted?
- Will I be teased or harassed because I smoke?

Cigarettes are expensive. They rob you of self-confidence, energy, a positive attitude, your time and your money. One of the activities listed at the end of this chapter enables to you estimate how much money you have spent as a smoker.

If you have no doubt in your mind and believe that what you say will happen, God will do it for you.

Mark 11: 23, The Answer

REMEMBERING PAST FAILURES

Even God can't undo the past, yet many of us wallow in guilt or regret when we think about the past. The awful reality of thinking about quitting is remembering past failures:

- I've been here before.
- I invested the energy and emotions in attempting to quit.
- "It" didn't work.

You may feel skeptical because you have:

- Trusted smoking cessation programs, products and/or instructors in the past, yet you were not successful in quitting;
- Never forgotten your disappointment of past failures to quit;
- Stopped believing in yourself.

One reason you may now hesitate to make another attempt to quit is unresolved frustration about previous unsuccessful tries. Thoughts of your past and memories of discomforts during the quitting process may repeatedly flash through your mind.

You may not understand why past quitting efforts didn't work. Or you may still feel blame or anger toward others associated with past failures. You may have feelings of doubt or anxiety when you remember how difficult quitting was during your previous attempts.

Learn from your past mistakes, then let go of them.

Return, faithless people; I will cure you of backsliding.

Jeremiah 3: 22, New International Version

LETTING GO OF PAST FAILURES

Sue Patton Thoele, author of many books, including *The Courage to Be Yourself* and *Freedoms after Fifty*, talks about those "dragon voices" – doubt and fear. When you think about quitting, do the voices of doubt and fear remind you of your past failures rather than your strengths and your faith in God?

It takes courage to say:
- I will let go of the past.
- I will forgive myself and anyone else I have blamed or resented.
- No matter how much I have smoked, my future is spotless.
- The past has passed.

There are three things you can do with your past smoking failures:
1.) Learn from your past mistakes and successfully quit now.
2.) Repeat unsuccessful efforts of the past, with the same failed result.
3.) Do nothing and remain an unhappy smoker, suffering the consequences.

Have you made any of these common mistakes in the past?
- Assuming there is only one "right" way to quit.
- Not talking to your physician about using a pharmaceutical product to make quitting easier.
- Waiting to quit until the time was "perfect".
- Engaging in self-sabotaging behavior (Example: deciding to quit smoking during what is already the most stressful time of your home or work schedule.)
- Making other people responsible for your failure.
- Having unreasonable expectations of the time needed to become a comfortable nonsmoker.
- Dwelling on past stop smoking mistakes, yet not learning from them.
- Quitting to please someone else, yet not feeling motivated or prepared.

The Lord is my light and my salvation; whom shall I fear? The Lord is the strength of my life; of whom shall I be afraid?

Psalm 27: 1, New King James Version

PUSHING FEAR AWAY

Before I quit I had many fears. Would I be able to write as well without a cigarette in my hand? When I experienced stress or unhappiness, what would I do instead of lighting up? Would I ever stop wanting a cigarette? With God's help and my efforts to love myself throughout the quitting process, I resolved every one of these issues – step by step by step.

Have you ever felt unable to move? Paralyzed by doubt and uncertainty? Immobilization can happen as a result of fear, when a person is afraid to risk new behavior or to think about setting new goals.

Fear is a natural reaction to change. It is probably the #1 reason people hesitate to make changes in their lives. Fear of the future and fear of failure keeps many people locked into a prison of their own making – unable or unwilling to change. Fear is high on the list of reasons why a smoker remains a smoker. A known misery may feel more acceptable than change and an unknown future.

Inside many adult smokers, the voice of fear says, "Why stop smoking? Live for today. Enjoy cigarettes. Tomorrow is not promised. Cigarettes are wonderful. Why quit?" Have you ever said that to yourself?

God never intended that you feel controlled by fear. The phrase "Fear not," appears frequently in the Bible. If you are feeling fear, might God be saying, "Move toward me and away from cigarettes? Transfer your dependence from nicotine to Me?"

Fear rears its ugly head often as a smoker prepares to quit, so be prepared. In moments of hunger, anger, stress, fatigue or confusion, fear stands at its tallest. When you are physically, mentally, emotionally or spiritually challenged, pay attention to what your body needs to function well: a close relationship with God, a healthy diet, sufficient sleep, relaxation and pleasure.

Be aware of your circumstances when you feel sad, lonely or disappointed. It is at these times that you are vulnerable to temptation and unhealthy "quick fixes". Those are the times to reach up to God. His strength overcomes any foe real or imagined. Fear of failure focuses on regrets, doubts and confusion: strategies the devil uses to divert believers from worthwhile God-centered goals and activities.

Now devote your heart and soul to seeking the Lord your God.

I Chronicles 22: 19, New International Version

KEEPING AN OPEN MIND TO GOD'S MESSAGE

You may be thinking: "I've tried to quit before, and it didn't work. I'd like to quit now, but I have no confidence that I'll be successful this time either." Doubts and lack of confidence are not unique issues.

God asked Moses to march into Pharaoh's court and confront him. Instead, Moses responded, "O Lord, please send someone else to do it."

When God asked Isaiah to volunteer for an important job, Isaiah cried, "Woe to me. I am ruined. For I am a man of unclean lips, and I live among a people of unclean lips."

Is God sending you a message to quit? Will your response be, "O, God, quitting is too difficult? I'd miss my cigarettes." Perhaps what God would like your response to be is, "With Your help, Heavenly Father, I will quit."

Noted therapist Elizabeth Kubler-Ross found that people who are terminally ill go through five identifiable psychological stages. These same basic steps, from denial to acceptance, also occur among most smokers who consider quitting:

Denial – that they are addicted to nicotine or that smoking is a serious problem in their lives.

Anger – at themselves, at nonsmokers or at the pressure they are feeling to quit.

Bargaining – by attempting to control their habit (i.e. I'll only smoke six cigarettes a day, or I'll only smoke "lite" cigarettes.)

Depression – often associated with low self-image that is made worse by an inability to quit smoking.

Acceptance – of the need to quit and the work needed to succeed.

Do any of these stage(s) describe your current emotions or behavior? Journal about issues that are unclear or troubling to you.

I am the Lord, and I do not change.

Malachi 3: 6, The Good News Bible

CHANGE: NOT EASY FOR MOST OF US

Change, which may eventually bring improved health and well being to smokers who quit, begins with what feels like bad news: different routines, different coping techniques and different ways of thinking and behaving.

Even smokers with a positive attitude who are determined to quit may battle with themselves. Cigarettes are as comforting as an old flannel bathrobe. And what is more familiar than coffee and a cigarette?

Change can be scary, unsettling and anxiety-producing. It can also be a challenging growth opportunity. Is it really possible for you to change how you feel about smoking – to realize that cigarettes are a dangerous enemy, not your best little buddy?

Yes, it is possible to have a complete change of heart. I have personally witnessed many long-time smokers who became very happy and comfortable nonsmokers. I feel confident that you too can be one of those success stories.

Do not deceive yourselves; no one makes a fool of God. A person will reap exactly what he plants.

Galatians 6: 7, The Good News Bible

BLAME VS. RESPONSIBILITY

Blaming yourself or feeling guilty for remaining a smoker is not the same thing as accepting responsibility. Blame, guilt and regret sap self-esteem and keep you a victim. It is only when you acknowledge a problem and accept responsibility for who you are and what you have done that you open the door to receive forgiveness and incorporate change.

Blame involves anger and judgment. If:

- It weren't for (fill in the blank).
- If only I hadn't (fill in the blank).
- Why didn't he or she (fill in the blank)?

Smokers who continue blaming circumstances or other people for their smoking are playing the Blame Game which:

- Is negative and destructive.
- Embraces denial and focuses on what other people did or failed to do.
- Is for immature people who like to argue or find excuses.
- Will not help a smoker become a nonsmoker.
- Is an energy-drainer that doesn't solve a thing.

If you have been playing the Blame Game, stop. Choose instead to display responsible, mature behavior.

A fool gives full vent to his anger, but a wise man keeps himself under control.

Proverbs 29: 11, New International Version

ANGER

Smokers often use a cigarette to diffuse, distract or deny themselves from the anger or frustration they may be feeling. (In the same manner, alcoholics or other substance abusers may reach for a drink or drugs to provide temporary relief for discomfort or a distraction from unhappiness.)

Anger is a frequent companion of many smokers, both when they are still smoking and certainly during the quitting process. Regardless of the motivation a smoker may have for deciding to quit, there is often a sense of loss and grief at the thought of losing one's cigarettes. And feelings of loss can open the door to anger.

Many smokers have a long history of not expressing their true feelings. There could be many reasons why that happened. Nicotine truly does provide a smoke screen to mask emotions or truths that the smoker may be afraid or unable to resolve through honest compromise and communication.

How can you determine whether anger management is a problem that you need to address? Reflect on the quality of your relationships with family and friends. If you frequently "fly off the handle", and later apologize or realize that those you've directed your anger toward feel intimidated or fearful, anger would seem to be an issue that you need to recognize and work to resolve.

We grow weak carrying burdens; there's so much rubble to take away.

Nehemiah 4: 10, Today's English Version

ACTIVITY: PUTTING A PRICE TAG
ON SMOKING COSTS

When I was a smoker, I often rationalized why it was okay to remain a smoker. I said to myself, "I work hard. I enjoy smoking. Therefore, I deserve to spend my money on cigarettes."

I rarely gave more than passing thought to how much money I spent on cigarettes and smoking related expenses. Maybe that is true for you too. While money may not be your primary reason for quitting, the amount of money you will save when you stop smoking can be a nice reward and an incentive to remain a nonsmoker.

To estimate the amount of money you spent last year on cigarettes and related costs, look at these possible expenses and total your expenditures:
- Cigarettes
- Cigarette lighters
- Cigarette carrying cases
- Ashtrays
- Over-the-counter products: throat lozenges, mouth wash
- Replacement of cigarette-burned: clothes, carpet, linoleum, car upholstery, furniture, countertops, _____
- Extra cleaning of: drapes, clothes, windows.
- More frequent interior painting in your house or apartment
- Additional insurance costs because you smoke: health, car, homeowners
- Lost revenue or vacation time due to smoking-related illnesses and doctor visits

To realize the total cost cigarettes may have cost you during your years of smoking, use the above list to estimate how much you have spent since you bought your first pack of cigarettes. Then, if you have not yet made the commitment to quit in the near future, project how much you would spend to remain a smoker during the years ahead.
- I estimate that I have already spent $_____ on smoking and smoking related expenses.
- If I continue to smoke for the next five years, I will spend an additional $_____.
- If I choose to quit, I could use my "cigarette money" on: _____.

Everything leads to weariness – a weariness too great for words. Our eyes can never see enough to be satisfied; our ears can never hear enough. What has happened before will happen again.

Ecclesiastes 1: 8-9, The Good News Bible

ACTIVITY: SORTING OUT THE JUNK

As you prepare to quit, think of ways you can make the quitting process less stressful. One helpful action is to look at ways to simplify daily patterns and tasks. Many people happily discover that once the "junk" in their lives is removed or reduced, life feels a whole lot easier.

Some of us have a lot of junk in our lives – physical or emotional clutter that makes it more difficult to focus on quitting smoking. Unnecessary "baggage" slows you down and complicates your life.

To sort out your junk, review daily activities and stresses. What could you give or throw away and probably not miss? What activities and obligations could you eliminate that would give you more hours to relax, rest or have fun?

Simultaneously, add as much self-care and positive rewards as possible. Think about what little joys you could add to give you pleasure and enjoyment. It might be as easy or frivolous as:

- Using the good dishes and table linens every day for the first month after quitting;
- Flying a kite;
- Taking a long tub bath;
- Wandering through a store you like;
- Reading your favorite newspaper section from cover to cover.

Choose not to use food, alcohol or any kind of drugs (legal, illegal or over-the-counter) as rewards, lest one bad habit is ended and a different one is embraced.

Ask, and it will be given to you; seek, and you will find; knock, and it will be opened to you. For everyone who asks receives, and he who seeks finds, and to him who knocks, it will be opened.

Matthew 7: 7-8, New King James Version

CHAPTER SIX: YOUR FIRST MONTH AS A NONSMOKER

❖

GOALS, AFFIRMATIONS & PRAYER

WHEN THINGS FEEL TOTALLY "OUT OF WHACK"

COPING DURING A CRISIS

WHEN TEMPTATION COMES CALLING

WHEN TEMPTATION COMES TO STAY

INTERNAL AND EXTERNAL ENEMIES

GOD'S PROMISES TO YOU

WANTING SUCCESS – NOW!

LISTENING TO YOUR BODY

AND IT CAME TO PASS

STAYING FOCUSED

ACTIVITY: LOOK FOR OPPORTUNITIES TO LIGHTEN UP

ACTIVITY: ELICIT THE SUPPORT YOU NEED

If God is for us, who can be against us?

Romans 8: 31, New King James Version

GOALS

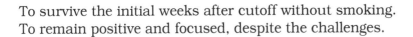

To survive the initial weeks after cutoff without smoking.
To remain positive and focused, despite the challenges.

AFFIRMATIONS

I feel God's presence and peace in my life, which enables me to appropriately handle any stress that might come into my life.
My days and nights are free from anxiety, doubt and fear.

PRAYER

God, you know how dependent I was on my cigarettes. Smoking was the first thing I wanted to do when I awoke, and the last thing I did before going to bed every night. The thought of life without cigarettes sometimes seems impossible.

It is easy for me to sink into self-pity. I think about what is missing in my life rather than feeling grateful for the many blessing that I so often take for granted. I ask that You help me to refocus my thoughts and attitude, Heavenly Father.

Calm me, Lord, and surround me with Your loving and strong presence. I need the confidence to know that with You, I can live far better without cigarettes. Help me to let go of dependence on cigarettes and to instead embrace Your love, strength and wisdom.
Amen

God is our refuge and strength, an ever-present help in trouble. Therefore, we will not fear, though the earth gives way and the mountains fall into the heart of the sea, though the waters roar and foam and the mountains quake with their surging.

Psalm 46: 1-3, New International Version

WHEN THINGS FEEL TOTALLY "OUT OF WHACK"

In *Faith in the Valley*, one of my favorite self-help authors, Iyanla Vanzant, said, "I once read that struggle, suffering and conflict are like magnets that draw us closer to God. It is not until we feel totally helpless, confused and sometimes desperate that we become willing or able to turn to the awesome power of life and living our Creator offers us."

In the immediate days after cut-off, smokers typically feel that they are stumbling through uncharted territory. There is an ever-present sense of things being totally "out of whack!" Be assured that it is natural to think about cigarettes often – perhaps many times every day. Maybe, many times every hour.

A new nonsmoker may fear never again feeling contented or in control. But remember that God remains your source of strength and love, despite the presence of turmoil, confusion or impatience. When you maintain control and choose not to smoke, praise and congratulate yourself for the success that you have demonstrated.

As you move through this "larva stage", visualize the beautiful butterfly that you will eventually become. Work to resolve any challenges you are experiencing, knowing that God is always with you. Trust Him to provide you with the strength that you need to get through whatever your battles and temptations are.

I, the Lord was there at the beginning, and I, the Lord God, will be there at the end.

Isaiah 41: 4, The Good News Bible

COPING DURING A CRISIS

Where can you turn when you're fearing or facing a crisis? In the recent past you probably lit a cigarette or two or three. Now that you are no longer smoking, consider the Bible an excellent source of strength and hope.

The Bible that I read most often is *The Daily Walk Bible*, published by Tyndale House Publishers, Inc. in Wheaton, Illinois. In one of the commentary sections, an unnamed writer counseled: "When life seems to be out of control and circumstances are as bewildering as a three-alarm fire, you have several options as to how you will respond. You can lean on your own strength and understanding, even though you have been warned not to. (Proverbs 3: 5).

Instead of reading the Bible, you could surround yourself with busyness or indulge yourself in a pleasure, but that probably won't remove your feelings of fear and inadequacy. Or you can ignore your problems and hope they go away, but chances are they may not.

A wise option would be to call upon the Lord, the only one who has promised never to leave you or forsake you (Matthew 28: 20; Hebrews 13: 5). It may sound like a simple solution – and in some ways it is. But with a Tower of Strength and Mercy like that awaiting your call twenty-four hours a day, why would anyone look elsewhere?"

Your feelings do not have to dictate your actions. Your emotions (and everyone else's) can and do turn on a dime. One minute you're feeling okay – the next minute you're feeling anxious or "jumpy". No one feels motivated, strong or self-controlled every minute of every day.

Remind yourself that having a cigarette won't change your circumstances in a positive way. If you choose to smoke, the same problems that existed before will still be there. All that will have changed is that you gave in to temptation rather than resisting it.

Happy is the person who remains faithful under trials, because when he succeeds in passing such a test, he will receive as his reward the life, which God has promised to those who love Him.

James 1: 12, The Good News Bible

WHEN TEMPTATION COMES CALLING

Yes, there will be temptations after you quit. There will be stress and perhaps those who try to sabotage your success. Yes, there may even be friends or family members offering you cigarettes. It isn't necessary to get angry with those people. Respond to your tempters by saying, "No, thank you. I no longer smoke."

Accept whatever happens. Deal with unsupportive people appropriately rather than wasting your time and energy wishing for the perfect environment.

Don't ignore temptation. Just choose not to focus on it. Instead, visualize being a comfortable, happy nonsmoker, remembering that no temptation has to be acted on. The thought of a cigarette may occur often. That doesn't mean you have to smoke one. Allow your commitment, not your temptations, to govern your behavior.

Former smokers, who seek to prove success to others by having "just one cigarette", are asking for trouble.

I have heard many unhappy smokers tell how they had once stopped smoking for long periods of time, then went to a party, wedding, funeral or other event and convinced themselves that one cigarette wouldn't hurt. They falsely believed that they could manage their smoking habit because they had gone for so long without cigarettes.

The typical story sounds like this: "So, a long time after I quit, I did the dumbest thing. I lit a cigarette and do you know what happened? Nothing. The sky didn't fall down, and I smoked just the one. So, several weeks later I bummed a cigarette from a friend, and again nothing dreadful happened. A few days later I bought a pack of cigarettes and thought, 'I'll just keep them on hand and have a cigarette once in a while. I honestly had no plans to resume smoking every day. But within one week I was right back up to my old two pack a day habit! Can you believe it?"

Yes, I do believe it, and I hope that you do too. One thing I want you to remember is that one cigarette WILL hurt.

We are tempted when we are drawn away and trapped by our own evil desires.

James 1: 14, The Good News Bible

WHEN TEMPTATION COMES TO STAY

How quickly the visions of success give way to the nitty gritty challenges of temptation. When temptation strikes and be assured that it will, be advised that denial and rationalization, (about having "just having one little cigarette"), may threaten to overcome days, weeks, months or even years of good judgment.

Temptation succeeds when you focus on short-term pleasures rather than on long-term consequences. The lure of temptation always focuses on the immediate benefits, not on the long-term negative results of "giving in" or giving up. There is a high price tag to pay for yielding to temptation: failure, lowered self-esteem, deep regret and perhaps compromising your life.

Be advised that the person who hated your smoking the most and who may have constantly nagged you to quit, may now be the same person who tempts you by saying:

- Well, aren't you the cranky one? Miss your cigarettes?
- I liked the old you (as a smoker) better.
- You never used to be angry all the time. Now you're impossible to live with.
- I can't believe that you're eating breakfast. When did that start?
- How much weight have you gained?

When you were a smoker, others may have used your smoking habit to manipulate or control you. However, once you quit and begin feeling and exhibiting more self-confidence, other people may feel less entitled to ridicule or humiliate you, thus losing the "hold" or power they once had.

An appropriate response to say to someone who sarcastically says, "You've changed!" would be: "Yes, I have. Thank you for noticing." Victory goes to the nonsmoker who perseveres for one minute more.

Help me, O Lord my God; because of your constant love, save me! Make my enemies know that you are the one who saves me. They may curse me, but you will bless me. May my persecutors be defeated, and may I, your servant, be glad.

Psalm 109: 26-28, The Good News Bible

INTERNAL AND EXTERNAL ENEMIES

In I Peter, the disciple urges Christians to endure external enemies with hope. In 2 Peter, he teaches them to oppose internal enemies with knowledge of the truth. These same two enemies — external and internal – exist today for smokers. And the same two weapons exist to overcome the enemies: hope and truth.

If I asked you to list the reasons you have been unable to quit in the past, your responses would typically be in one of those same two categories:

External Enemies
- Other smokers
- Stress, "real" or perceived
- Fear of or the reality of weight gain
- Substance abuse (alcohol and/or drugs)
- Insufficient sleep
- Skipping meals

Internal Issues
- Lack of perseverance or self-discipline
- Anger
- Boredom
- Loneliness
- Complacency (I've got my problem – smoking – under control.)

Internal enemies, often unknown or unacknowledged by the smoker, can be more potent because they are usually hidden or deeply ingrained issues that extend beyond smoking. Hope and truth, in Jesus Christ, coupled with hard work and perseverance, are the best antidotes.

The Sovereign Lord says, "See, I lay a stone in Zion, a tested stone, a precious cornerstone for a sure foundation; the one who trusts will never be dismayed.

Isaiah 28: 16, New International Version

GOD'S PROMISES TO YOU

Computer manufacturers knew that some users would have difficulty remembering the what's, how's and when's as they worked toward becoming computer literate. That must have been why, in their great foresight, they integrated a "HELP" function key.

God, our Heavenly Father, is always available, as our "24-7" Heavenly HELP resource. He is there for you during difficult moments. God is also there during times of rest and relaxation, when He will refresh and renew your body, soul and spirit.

Quitting smoking is the perfect time to turn cares, worries and addictions over to God, knowing that while you don't have all the answers or power, God does. He has promised that He will provide for all of His children's needs, and He does.

During the cutoff phase, remember that while some things in life are within human control, many others are not. Choose to plan ahead and be prepared. Also, choose to be flexible and physically rested to better cope with the outside stresses and temptations. As you change and your emotions adjust, know that God remains stable, steady and secure to strengthen you.

Jesus told them, "You don't get to know the time. Timing is the Father's business. What you'll get is the Holy Spirit."

Acts 1: 7-8, The Message

WANTING SUCCESS – NOW!

Often, a new nonsmoker wistfully or angrily says, "I sure wish I felt more comfortable about not smoking. I am not there yet". These are understandable feelings. You may not be there yet, but if you're still not smoking, you are closer to success today than you were yesterday. Be patient. Set realistic expectations.

Changing behavior can bring out the worst moods in anyone. By definition a habit is a thing that is done often and usually done easily. Change on the other hand denotes making adjustments or becoming distinctly different.

Change begins with making a commitment to yourself. But you don't decide just once to quit smoking. Many times in the days that follow, your actions will determine whether you remain a nonsmoker. Every time you think about or desire a cigarette, you have a choice to make: Do I smoke or not?

I have heard thousands of stories from former smokers, some describing their victories, others their defeats. In 2001 I met a woman in Clarksville, Missouri who proudly described how she had once quit smoking for six months.

Then she learned that one of her children was divorcing. The sadness of this family crisis was the excuse she gave to herself and others for returning to cigarettes. Of course, nothing positive occurred when she resumed smoking. Her son still divorced, and the woman who had once celebrated six months of nonsmoking was right back where she started.

The moral of the story is that it doesn't matter how initially motivated or successful a smoker is. It's the finishing that counts.

Lord, heal me and I will be completely well; rescue me and I will be perfectly safe. You are the one I praise.
Jeremiah 17:14, The Good News Bible

LISTENING TO YOUR BODY

Cigarettes aren't the only automatic habit some people practice. Some mature adults continue eating unhealthy food (and perhaps too much of it) or maybe try getting by with far less sleep or exercise than their body needs. Others drink too much alcohol or rely on pills to sleep, lose weight or maybe to lift their spirits.

Treat your body with as much respect and tender loving care as an Olympic athlete in training would.

It has been estimated that only 42 percent of Americans eat breakfast every day of the week. My personal observation is that those who smoke more than one pack a day usually either skip breakfast or do not eat until they have been up for three or more hours.

Eat something within an hour after you get up. Your body needs food! Do not skip any meals. Do not go more than five hours between meals. Eat healthy, low calorie snacks between meals.

Drink lots of water – ideally eight 8-ounce glasses a day. Water is essential to good health and is an excellent appetite suppressant. It's also great for you skin. Don't wait until feeling thirsty before drinking water. The human body usually doesn't recognize dehydration.

Sleep is one of the regenerative gifts of life. A person can't think clearly, work effectively or function above the robot level if chronically deprived of sufficient sleep.

And naps? They are one of life's little blessings. When you've got a lot of things to do, it's always a good idea to get the nap out of the way first.

But he who stands firm to the end will be saved.

Matthew 24: 13, New International Version

AND IT CAME TO PASS

The immediate goal during the first few days after cutoff is just getting through each urge to smoke: not smoking for the next ten minutes. Each hour that a person survives without a cigarette is to be acknowledged and celebrated.

Be assured that the thought of a cigarette will pass if you distract yourself and do or think about something else. If you are feeling anxious or sad, remember that Christ is the answer to emptiness and sorrow.

When Harry Lauder, a Scottish entertainer, learned that his son had been killed, he said, "In a time like this, there are three courses open to man: He may give way to despair and become bitter. He may endeavor to drown his sorrow in drink or in a life of wickedness. Or he may turn to God."

One man explained that his favorite phrase in the Bible was "And it came to pass." Trouble may come, but at least it doesn't stay. It comes to pass.

Allow time to integrate lifestyle change knowing that your cigarette-related challenges will pass. Be patient and remind yourself that recovery is not a race or a competition with anyone.

Watch out that you do not lose what you have worked for, but that you may be rewarded fully.

2 John 8, New International Version

STAYING FOCUSED

The main thing is to keep the main thing the main thing.
– Author Unknown

Are you feeling overwhelmed by the amount of energy it takes to remain a nonsmoker? If you are, remind yourself (as often as needed) that the vast majority of the other "stuff" in your life will be forgotten six months from now. I guarantee you that you will either remember with pride that you quit or with regret that you didn't.

Daily remind yourself that the main thing in your life is remaining a nonsmoker. It is easy to get distracted by other issues or to feel overwhelmed by your changing lifestyle during the first weeks as a nonsmoker. Choose to remember that:

- A car can only travel in one direction at a time. That is also true of your mind and body.
- There are many clothes in most closets, yet a person wears only one outfit at a time.

In the same manner, there are many issues in everyone's life. Right now, choose to maintain your major focus on one issue: remaining a nonsmoker. As other issues surface, trust that God will provide you with the ability, energy and knowledge to complete the important things and to discard or postpone the rest.

"The main thing is to keep the main thing the main thing."

Stay focused on what you have learned. Reread sections of this book for motivation and encouragement. You have all the strength and knowledge to be successful. All of the power and energy are within your grasp. You + God = Success.

He who sits in the heavens shall laugh.

Psalms 2:4, Revised Standard Version

ACTIVITY: LOOK FOR OPPORTUNITIES TO LIGHTEN UP

Some smokers who quit are so cranky, joyless and intense that even the people who truly love them want to be somewhere else. Just because you're not lighting up doesn't mean you can't lighten up.

Living without laughter, without seeing the humor and irony during all of life's experiences, is unthinkable. This is especially true during the quitting process, despite the fact that you may have never felt less like laughing or being silly.

For many people, laughter comes easily during light-hearted, happy moments. But, consider that laughter provides even greater benefits during times of challenges.

Think about what you can do to have fun today. Do not worry about what others think. No person is too old, too successful or too sophisticated for "such nonsense". Playfulness is a built-in stress reducer and has many faces. Exactly how and when it demonstrates itself in each individual is unique.

Consider enjoying a humorous movie, video, audiotape or book. If you are blessed to have a friend who can always make you laugh, contact that person today. If you don't have a person like that in your life, watch a silly sitcom on television or read the comics.

Keep company with the wise and you will become wise. If you make friends with stupid people, you will be ruined.

Proverbs 13; 20, The Good News Bible

ACTIVITY: ELICIT THE SUPPORT YOU NEED

When I am going through a rough time, I tend to isolate and try to work out the issues on my own. Sometimes that approach works but sometimes the more I dwell on a problem the bigger it seems to become.

Is it difficult for you to admit when you need help? Consider asking a friend for encouragement or to just listen if you feel like talking.

Regrettably, many smokers preparing to quit do not have loving, supportive people around them during the quitting process. Some people are single, living alone or without close friends or family.

Others may be in unhappy or broken families or relationships that drain, rather than support them. Yet other smokers might have a mate or close person in their lives who continues to smoke and who may resent the smoker's decision to quit.

For those persons quitting who do not have a friend to provide the support that they feel they need, here are some suggestions that you might choose to try:

* Read your Bible or other Christian books;
* Spend some time identifying your emotional issues, especially any anger that you may be holding on to;
* Write a letter or in a diary, describing any frustrations, sadness or resentment to release the feelings that cause pain;
* Consider seeking professional counseling.

Call to me, and I will answer you; I will tell you wonderful and marvelous things that you know nothing about.

Jeremiah 33: 3, The Good News Bible

CHAPTER SEVEN: ISSUES DURING THE TRANSITIONAL PHASE

GOALS, AFFIRMATIONS & PRAYER

MEDITATION, PRAYER AND BIBLE READING

COPING

PERSEVERANCE

ISOLATION FOLLOWING CUTOFF

LONELINESS

REWARDS

MAINTAINING BALANCE IN YOUR LIFE

ACTIVITY: MAKING A GOD JAR

ACTIVITY: SPEAKING KINDLY TO YOURSELF

About the time everybody's walking around complacently, con-
gratulating each other – "We've sure got it made! Now we can take
it easy!" – suddenly everything will fall apart. It's going to happen
as suddenly and inescapably as birth pangs to a pregnant woman.
But friends, you're not in the dark, so how could you be taken off
guard by any of this?

I Thessalonians 5: 3-4, The Message

GOALS

Recognizing the importance of prayers and meditation in daily life. Persevering through the challenges and problems that present themselves during the quitting process.

AFFIRMATIONS

- I am filled with God's strength and love. He hears my prayers and knows my fears.
- I appreciate God's gifts of perseverance and faith. I receive healing in my mind, body and spirit.
- I accept that growth and change involve processes that take time.
- I feel confident enough to reach out to others when I feel lonely, sad or fearful.
- I will survive and be stronger as a result of quitting, healing and changing.

PRAYER

Almighty and gracious God, during this time of my life, may I demonstrate courage and confidence instead of despair. May I remember that I have a Savior who brings strength out of faith, blessings out of struggle, and victory out of perseverance. Help me to be fearful of nothing, secure in the knowledge that I am safely protected in Your loving care. Amen

So He (Jesus) said to them, "Let us go off by ourselves to some place where we will be alone.

Mark 6: 31, The Good News Bible

MEDITATION, PRAYER AND BIBLE READING

Meditation and prayer can be particularly helpful during the stop smoking process. For those who are struggling and sometimes wonder who they are, what they want or where they are going, devoting time to spiritual needs can provide you with direction and peace.

Even in a busy, stress-filled life, you can find solace and joy. In fact, the more demanding your schedule, the more essential it is for you to take daily spiritual breaks to renew and refresh yourself.

I highly recommended that you have a specific place and a defined time for prayers, meditation and Bible reading. Spend at least fifteen minutes daily reading spiritual books, talking with God and listening for His responses.

For most people, the first hour after arising offers an ideal opportunity for spiritual growth. It's a great way to start the day, even if it means setting the alarm clock for an earlier wake-up time. Meditation, prayer and Bible reading provide both motivation and serenity.

Find a comfortable and quiet spot. Bring along a pen and a cup of coffee, tea, juice or water and a journal in which to write.

Begin by closing your eyes and inviting the presence of God, through the Holy Spirit, to guide and sustain you. As your mind is quieted, release any negative thoughts or feelings of helplessness or hopelessness.

Be prepared to receive a "high" unlike any you have ever received from nicotine.

God, save me! I'm in over my head. Quicksand under me, swamp water over me; I'm going down for the third time.

Psalm 69: 1-2, The Message

COPING

There may be conditions and people in your life who are generating feelings of stress, anger or frustration. That's just the way life is. I don't know anyone who has a perfectly serene life. You can choose to feel angry about that reality or you can choose to change it, accept it or cope with it. While the stress in your life may remain the same, a change in your attitude can make it tolerable.

What are the first things you do when your life seems turned upside down?

Get upset? Angry? Blame someone or something for the problems? Immediately think about "resolving" the problems, in the same old unsatisfactory way you always used: by reaching for a cigarette?

All of us are creatures of habit, who automatically think about old patterns of behavior. Now is a good time to ask yourself, "What could be a better response to my problems than thinking about or having a cigarette?"

- Acknowledge the pain, anger or discomfort – the first step in resolving or successfully coping with the problem.
- Accept the fact that life sometimes is unfair.
- Choose to maintain a positive attitude, despite your circumstances.
- Practice coping techniques of acceptance and relaxation.

Tolerance is a key concept during the recovery process. Tolerate:

- Mood swings.
- The imperfect world in which we live.
- The process of quitting.

After mastering tolerance, acceptance is the next goal. Tolerance may involve clenched teeth, white knuckles and a churning stomach. Acceptance embraces the truth with serenity of mind, body and spirit.

We will reap a harvest if we do not give up.

Galatians 6: 9, New International Version

PERSEVERANCE

Sometimes quitting seems overwhelming. The process is too long, too stressful and too demanding. There are moments of doubt and times of fear that the stop smoking goal cannot be maintained. These feelings are normal. Respond by just getting through the moment.

What is your first instinct when you face a challenge or unwelcome stress? Flight? Instant escape may sound very appealing. Yet God, in His infinite wisdom, teaches us to face problems instead of running away or looking for a quick fix.

Perseverance pays off. Giving up is not part of God's plan for His children. Pray for the tenacity and perseverance to complete the stop smoking process. Choose to hang in there, despite the challenges and resistance. Travel the full path, knowing that there are no shortcuts to success.

Few new habits feel normal right away. Yet occasionally, even mature adults feel like whiny little kids – rejecting, pouting and complaining about what they don't want to do. It will not feel natural to be a nonsmoker right away. Don't expect it to. But the day will come, I promise, when you will feel happy and proud that you persevered.

For the Spirit that God has given us does not make us timid; instead, His Spirit fills us with power, love and self-control.

2 Timothy 1: 7, The Good News Bible

ISOLATION FOLLOWING CUTOFF

Many people isolate during difficult times. It can feel embarrassing to admit weakness or fear to others. Although there are many advantages in reaching out for support, who wants to say?

- I am struggling!
- I don't know if I can do this.
- I need help.

Those kinds of confessions are admissions that you don't have all the answers.

Smokers who remain physically, spiritually or emotionally isolated are far more vulnerable to feelings of anger, sadness or self-pity. They are also more likely to distort reality, thinking that nobody cares or that there is no one to whom they can turn for support and encouragement.

One of the reasons people feel despair is that they don't ask for help. Asking for what it is needed is a sign of maturity, not weakness.

The Lord is my rock and my fortress and my deliverer, the God of my strength, in whom I will trust; my shield and the horn of my salvation, my stronghold and my refuge; my Savior, you saved me from violence. I will call upon the Lord, who is worthy to be praised, so will I be saved from my enemies.

2 Samuel 22: 2-4, New King James Version

LONELINESS

Feeling lonely is common during cutoff. This is especially true of smokers who regarded their cigarettes as their "best little buddy".

During difficult times, you can receive great solace by reminding yourself that God loves you and is with you, even when you feel cranky and doubt His presence; even when you are whiny and feel all alone.

The devil camps out in the mind of a person with doubts and fears and knows all of your vulnerabilities. He will stalk you relentlessly, reminding you of your past failures, whispering, "Where is this god of yours when you need him?" Of course the devil's greatest desire is to possess the hearts of God's children.

Remember: God has promised that He will never abandon you. If you feel lonely, reach out to God and to loyal Christian friends. There is a wonderful hymn called, "Lean on Me". God never intended that you face life's struggles and temptations alone.

Paul's advice in Colossians 2: 6-7 (The Message) is to urge Christians to continue working hard, knowing that they are not alone. "My counsel for you is simple and straightforward: Just go ahead with what you have been given. Now do what you have been taught. School's out; quit studying the subject and start living it!"

The Bible is intended to be your personal resource guide. I enjoy reading different versions, as perhaps you have noticed from the various translations that I have included in this book. Read the Bible, write notes in the margins and draw strength from the God's Word.

Each one will receive his own reward according to his own labor.

I Corinthians 3: 8, New King James Version

REWARDS

Most smokers think of cigarettes as "little rewards" that they give themselves when they complete a project or push down a "negative" emotion. They have a cigarette after they:

- Finish a report
- Mow the yard
- Mop the floor

They "deserve" a cigarette because they didn't:

- Yell at their kids
- Argue with their neighbors
- Honk at the drivers who cut them off in traffic

After cut-off it is only natural to miss the little "rewards" (cigarettes). This is often when smokers who recently quit are tempted to substitute food, alcohol or another "quick fix" for cigarettes.

Now is the perfect time for you to enjoy rewards that appeal to one of your other senses: sight, touch, sound and smell. When you enjoy healthy, life-affirming rewards, you are less likely to think about cigarettes.

Consider including some of these rewards:

- A walk, physical workout or workout at a health club
- Model trains or cars
- Tennis, bowling, fishing or racquetball
- A new Bible or spiritual book
- Special bath soap or gel
- Large fluffy towels
- Watching a sporting event, live or on television
- Soft new sheets
- Fresh flowers
- A designated time to play with your children, grandchildren or pets
- Golf or archery

This is the day of the Lord's victory; let us be happy, let us celebrate.

Psalm 118: 24, The Good News Bible

MAINTAINING BALANCE IN YOUR LIFE

Balance is always a key concept.

Persons, who focus exclusively on self-growth and self-improvement, deciding they are too busy or too old to laugh and have fun, won't enjoy themselves very much and neither will anyone else. Amid all the self-discovery and self-discipline that accompany stopping smoking, don't forget to have fun.

The third chapter of Ecclesiastes (Everything that happens in this world happens at the time God chooses....) talks about the importance of balance in our lives. This is particularly true during the quitting process.

I WANT TO STOP SMOKING ... SO HELP ME GOD! talks about the value of maintaining balance, in part by promoting values and activities that may at first seem like opposites:

- WORKING the programs & WAITING for long-term success;
- Physical ACTIVITY & calming deep BREATHING;
- WORKING on new behaviors & REFLECTING on God's presence;
- DO-ing & BE-ing

Choose to maintain balance in your life.

But you are a chosen generation, a royal priesthood, a holy nation, His own special people, that you may proclaim the praises of Him who called you out of darkness into His marvelous light.

I Peter 2: 9, New King James Version

ACTIVITY: MAKING A GOD JAR

Make a God Jar – a container in which written prayers for guidance in troublesome situations are placed. A large mayonnaise or pickle jar is the ideal size. This activity provides a specific and symbolic form of "turning it over". It makes the act of surrender an active leap of faith.
(This idea is from Julia Cameron's, *God Is No Laughing Matter*.)

If you write about a problem you are having, you have a record of it. It is then no longer necessary for you to continually rehash the same conflicts in your mind. What are the advantages of replaying your fears and doubts unless they are helping you resolve a problem? Continually thinking about your challenges only reinforce a sense of failure or can cause you to feel depressed.

Instead, think about the successes you intend to experience. Picture in your mind how proud and happy you will feel. And know that God can handle any of the problems you turn over to Him.

Your prayers to God might include specific concerns such as:

- I especially need Your help when ...
- I still struggle with ...
- Lord, my automatic response is to look for my cigarettes whenever I feel angry or frustrated.
- Comfort me during difficult moments, such as ....
- Help me, God, not to reach for food every time I think about smoking.

Love your neighbor as you love yourself.

James 2: 8, The Good News Bible

ACTIVITY: SPEAK KINDLY TO YOURSELF

Self-love is essential, especially during the transitional phase. Thinking negative thoughts about yourself is self-sabotage. Why would you want to send self-destructive messages to your mind or body?

You are a precious child of God, loved by God unconditionally. Choose to embrace that same unconditional love for yourself. Positive messages to yourself = positive results for yourself.

Negative messages = negative results.

Other people also receive and respond in like fashion to negative messages. If you frequently make negative remarks about yourself, regardless of the reasons, do not be surprised if others also devalue you in thought, word or deed.

Instead of being self-critical, focus on your strengths. Think and say positive things to yourself and about yourself and believe them.

Affirmations
* Regardless of what I have done or failed to do, I am a good person worthy of love and respect.
* With God's help and direction, I will follow the plan He has for my life.
* Failures in my past can now serve as a flashlight to point out areas I choose to address.

The Lord spoke to me, "Mortal man," he said, "you are living among rebellious people. They have eyes, but they see nothing; they have ears, but they hear nothing because they are rebellious."

Ezekiel 12: 1-2, The Good News Bible

CHAPTER EIGHT: REMAINING A NONSMOKER

❖

GOALS, AFFIRMATIONS & PRAYER

MORE ON WORK AND PERSEVERANCE

CONFIDENCE VS. WORRY

LIVING THROUGH THE TRANSITION

THE DIFFERENCE BETWEEN SUCCESS & FAILURE

AN ATTITUDE OF GRATITUDE

A PUFF AWAY FROM A PACK A DAY

ACTIVITY: TALKING WITH GOD

ACTIVITY: INTEGRATING CHRISTIANITY WITH QUITTING

But He (Jesus) said to me, "My grace is sufficient for you, for my power is made perfect in weakness."

2 Corinthians 12: 9, Revised Standard Version

GOAL

To persevere throughout the quitting process, however long or challenging that period of time may be.
To focus on the benefits of quitting and let go of any remaining emotional ties to cigarettes.

AFFIRMATIONS

Today God will reveal some of His plan and wisdom to me, as well as His strategies to lessen any pain and sadness that I feel. Success will be mine if I choose to remain in control and not smoke.

PRAYER

Grant me, O Heavenly Father, Your peace, which passes all under-standing, for I am sometimes burdened by temptations, troubles and cranky moods. Soothe and calm me, assuring me that I am in Your care and embraced by Your love. Help me to accept that with a trusting heart, I can face the storms of life, through Jesus Christ my Lord and my Redeemer. Amen.

Anyone who starts to plow and then keeps looking back is no use for the Kingdom of God.

Luke 9: 62, The Good News Bible

MORE ON WORK AND PERSEVERANCE

"Stick-to-it-ness": remaining true in actions to what is verbally committed. Perseverance is a gold-plated characteristic of a successful quitter.

It is easy for a smoker to say: "I want to quit smoking." It is now your challenge and opportunity to consistently follow that desire with actions. Failure usually occurs when someone quits working or loses sight of the goal. Those who succeed are those who persevere, even when feeling discouraged. Winners fight through fatigue, boredom and discomfort.

Almost every smoker struggles during the quitting process, and you probably will too. For days, weeks or even months, it may seem as if there is no progress in your moods or attitude, despite your efforts. Your desire for a cigarette may still feel strong. As a new nonsmoker, you may occasionally or frequently wallow in self-pity.

But, if you choose to abstain from smoking, the day will come when the cravings for a cigarette will subside, then end.

The quitting process is unique for each smoker. Recovery follows its own path and time line. For the person who is quitting, feeling comfortable as a nonsmoker may seem to take forever. It is often easier to focus on the frustrations and challenges you are experiencing than on the progress and changes that you have made but perhaps not acknowledged.

Most of us want any major change we decide on to be effortless and fast. But, remind yourself that quitting is a process, and each day brings you closer to feeling comfortable as a person who no longer smokes.

God, my God, I yelled for help and you put me together. God, you pulled me out of the grave, gave me another chance at life when I was down and out.

Psalm 30: 2, The Message

CONFIDENCE VS. WORRY

It's understandable if you feel discouraged.

Remind yourself that every ex-smoker got to where he or she is after surviving what you are now experiencing. Don't give up. For the first few months after quitting, expect that your moods and emotions may be up one minute and down the next. You are in what might be called the roller coaster phase.

Sometimes you will feel calm and confident from what you have learned and achieved. During these times, you may feel at peace and in control. Celebrate these positive moments and express gratitude to God.

At other moments, you may feel anxious and uncertain. There may be times when it feels impossible to be positive, much less cheerful.

Mood swings are normal and to be expected during the roller coaster phase. Accept that life always offers joy and challenges, laughter and despair, in the same way that there is sunshine and rain, blue skies and fog.

Your goal to become a confident nonsmoker may have speed bumps along the way. Fear and worry may continue to surface, eating away at your resolve. But, as you continue not to smoke, your feelings of self-confidence will increase, and your fears will diminish.

Gradually you will have fewer thoughts about having a cigarette and more feelings of gratitude and pride.

At all times carry faith as a shield; for with it you will be able to put out all the burning arrows shot by the Evil One.

Ephesians 6: 16, Today's English Version

LIVING THROUGH THE TRANSITION

When anyone is in the middle of a painful transition, sadness or despair can seem unending. A person may think: Will this misery ever be over? Will there ever be the feeling that my life is "normal" again?

Is this how you are feeling?

Think back to other transitional times you may have experienced: a difficult class, sadness felt when moving to a new school, neighborhood or job; suffering through an illness, accident or hospitalization; surviving the teenaged years; the heartbreak of a broken relationship; death of a loved one.

In retrospect, does it seem that despite the difficulty, you survived and learned a great deal as a result of your crisis or challenge? That what seemed to be such a negative experience eventually evolved into strength, wisdom gained or perhaps even a positive turning point in your life?

As you reflect and work through difficulties, hold fast to your faith in God. Choose to grow and mature as a result of what you have learned. Look for the rainbow in the thunderstorm and feel God's presence.

One day the fog will lift, and your recovery will be complete.

But they did not listen or pay attention; instead, they followed the stubborn inclinations of their evil hearts. They went backward and not forward.

Jeremiah 7: 24, New International Version

THE DIFFERENCE BETWEEN
SUCCESS AND FAILURE

When an admirer questioned the accomplished pianist Ignace Paderewski if he still practiced every day, he replied, "Yes, at least six hours a day". The admirer responded, "You have a world of patience". "No," Paderewski replied, "I have no more patience than anyone else. I just use mine".

What is the difference between success and failure? Sometimes surprisingly little. Success may simply call for:

- One minute more;
- Saying no, one more time, to temptation;
- Hanging in there rather than giving up.

Beethoven is said to have rewritten each bar of his music at least ten times.

Joseph Haydn wrote more than 800 pieces of music before producing "The Creation", the oratorio for which he is most famous.

Michelangelo's "Last Judgment" painting took eight years to complete.

Leonardo da Vinci worked on his famous painting "The Last Supper" for ten years.

Patience, endurance and perseverance separate winners and losers. It isn't that those who successfully stop smoking found the process to be easy. They just hung in there.

People who persevere up deserve the success they achieve.

Be thankful in all circumstances.

I Thessalonians 5: 17, The Good News Bible

AN ATTITUDE OF GRATITUDE

Melody Beattie, in her book, *The Language of Letting Go,* urges her readers to, "Say thank you until you mean it. Thank God ... for everyone and everything sent your way. Gratitude unlocks the fullness of life. It turns what we have into enough and more. It turns denial into acceptance, chaos into order, confusion to clarity....

It turns problems into gifts, failures into successes.... Gratitude makes sense of our past, brings peace for today and creates a vision for tomorrow. Gratitude makes things right."

Today, give thanks to God for His guidance and for opening the door to improved health and a better life as a nonsmoker.

Do not say, "I'll thank God when ...." That's trying to bargain with or blackmail God. He is already on your side. For those who are not feeling His presence, there may be fear, insecurity or resistance, but be assured: God is with you.

Continue to thank God for each day of success. When you show your gratitude, you are turning over the controls to the Father, acknowledging His presence, influence and power and releasing your fears and doubts.

Come back to your right senses and stop your sinful ways.

I Corinthians 15; 34, The Good News Bible

A PUFF AWAY FROM A PACK A DAY

You are a puff away from a pack a day.

All the hard work invested in quitting can be undone by one puff on a cigarette. Believe this. Choose to not sabotage your success.

If you should "slip", acknowledge your mistake. Immediately "get back on the wagon" and vow to be better prepared to resist temptation the next time it strikes. Know what times, places and moments are your trigger situations. Plan ahead and avoid known temptations.

Mistakes happen. That's why Jesus talked about forgiveness. People who give in to temptation often feel the shame and pain of defeat. But everyone, like Peter, who denied Jesus three times, can immediately realize a misjudgment and get back on the right track. Forgive yourself and let go of the mistake. Learn from the incident. Do not dwell on it.

But be clear about the long-term consequences of repeating the same mistake. Recovery from a slip or two is possible. But the greater the number and frequency of the slips, the lower the probability of you achieving success as a nonsmoker.

And remember, I am with you always, to the end of the age.

Matthew 28: 20, Today's English Version

ACTIVITY: TALKING WITH GOD

If anyone is experiencing pain, frustration, loneliness, pain and feeling that no one knows and no one cares, hold a cordless phone and have a long call with God.

Go into great deal of detail about your situation. Your friends and family might be bored or uncomfortable with what you share about your quitting challenges, but God won't.

Express any anger you may be feeling. Ask for wisdom. It's okay to scream, whine, cry or whimper. Remember that God has your name written in the palm of His hand. He even knows how many hairs are on your head. God listens to you, loves you and accepts every one of your messages unconditionally.

What a Heavenly Father!

If we claim to be without sin, we deceive ourselves and the truth is not in us. If we confess our sins, he is faithful and just and will forgive us our sins and purify us from all unrighteousness.

I John 1: 8 – 9, New International Version

ACTIVITY: INTEGRATING CHRISTIANITY WITH QUITTING

❖

Smokers who "live their faith", don't have to fight the battles alone. Yet, some Christians think of faith as something that stays inside church. For Sunday-only-Christians, faith is confessed and shared within a safe, defined Christian congregation, but Monday through Saturday their faith is buried or denied.

Christianity is meant to be lived, used and practiced seven days a week. That is the way that God intended for us to relate to him: every day, in every situation. Being a Sunday-only Christian makes as much sense as eating one day a week.

Consider including these Christian activities in your recovery process:

❖ Ask Christian friends for their prayers.
❖ Write Bible promises that tell of God's love in a small notebook that you carry and regularly read.
❖ Listen to Christian radio programs or Christian music.

Enjoy all of the benefits, pleasures and strengths by being a 24/7 Christian.

Even though the fig trees have not fruit and no grapes grow on the vines, even though the olive crop fails and the fields produce no grain, even though the sheep all die and the cattle stalls are empty, I will still be joyful and glad, because the Lord God is my savior. The Sovereign Lord gives me strength. He makes me sure-footed as a deer and keeps me safe on the mountains.

Habakkuk 3: 17-19, The Good News Bible

CHAPTER NINE: INFORMATION AND SUGGESTIONS FOR NONSMOKERS

❖

GOALS, AFFIRMATIONS & PRAYER

IS THERE ANY WAY I (A NONSMOKER) CAN CONVINCE
A SMOKER TO QUIT?

SUGGESTIONS FOR NONSMOKERS

COPING, AS A NONSMOKER

ISSUES NONSMOKERS MAY HAVE NOT CONSIDERED

WHAT A NONSMOKER CAN DO TO BE SUPPORTIVE
OF A SMOKER WHO CHOOSES TO QUIT

SUGGESTIONS FOR HEALTH CARE PROFESSIONALS

ACTIVITY: HOW I CAN SUPPORT MY SMOKER

ACTIVITY: IF MY SMOKER SHOULD EVER THINK
ABOUT QUITTING

I have the strength to face all conditions by the power that Christ gives me.

Philippians 4: 13, The Good News Bible

GOALS

Educating nonsmokers who live with or medically treat smokers about how smokers think and respond to suggestions of quitting. Providing information and suggestions for nonsmokers so that they can better cope with smoking-related challenges.

AFFIRMATIONS

My values and needs, as a nonsmoker, have merit and deserve respect, as do smokers' values and needs.
My voice, as a nonsmoker, is more likely to be heard if I present my thoughts in a genuinely loving voice and nonjudgmental manner.

PRAYER

Lord Jesus Christ, You experienced rejection, betrayal and desertion by Your disciples, friends and followers. Your prayers sometimes went unanswered, just as mine have when I've prayed that my loved one would quit smoking.

When I feel the pain and sadness that You must have felt, please give me the faith that You had in the Father. I need and ask for the assurance of Your wisdom, strength and love, regardless of the smoker's decision or the outcome, should the smoker attempt to quit. In Your name I pray. Amen.

With God all things are possible.
Matthew 19: 26, New International Version

IS THERE ANY WAY I (A NONSMOKER) CAN CONVINCE A SMOKER TO QUIT?

Smokers can essentially be put into one of three categories:

1.) Those who love their cigarettes and have no interest in quitting. Leave Them Alone. Efforts to convince them to quit, at least at this time, are futile. Discussions about quitting will only aggravate them and you.

2.) Those who realize that they are addicted to cigarettes but talk about quitting. These smokers may say that they would quit if they only knew how.

3.) Those who seem indifferent to the idea of quitting. They continue smoking and don't want to talk about quitting. Indifferent people seldom lack knowledge. Rather, they lack a willingness to address the smoking issue. They choose (literally) to keep their heads in the clouds.

Step one of Alcoholics Anonymous says, "We admitted that we were powerless."

Nonsmokers are also powerless – unable to make a smoker quit. You may have already tried threats, blackmail, intellectualizing or educating someone about the dangers of smoking. Seldom do any of these strategies work.

Only the smoker can decide whether or not to quit. Listen to and believe what the smoker says. If the smoker says, "I'll never quit!" an appropriate response would be, "Is that because you don't want to quit or because you don't think you can quit?"

If the smoker doesn't want to quit, believe and accept the decision.

If, on the other hand, the smoker wants to quit and doesn't know how, you might give him or her this book as suggested reading.

He who ignores discipline despises himself, but whoever heeds correction gains understanding.

Proverbs 16: 32, New International Version

SUGGESTIONS FOR NONSMOKERS

If what you have said to the smoker has not changed the smoker's behavior in the past, is there any reason for you to believe that the smoker will now become enlightened and decide that you are right?

Likewise, it makes no sense for you to cry, nag, threaten or bargain. Do not withhold love, sex or rewards. Attempts to control or manipulate the smoker into quitting have not and will not work, regardless of your motivation — regardless of how "right" you might be. Focus instead on how to best react to the smoker and the smoking.

Choose not to start arguments. You can be strong and honest about your anti-smoking convictions without seeking agreement from the smoker. It is OK for you to feel passionately against smoking, just as it is OK for smokers to resent anyone's attempts to change them. Agree to disagree, without using shame, guilt or anger.

Choose to set mutually agreeable boundaries with the smoker. For example the smoker might agree not to smoke:
- In the car,
- Bedroom, or
- In the nonsmoker's presence.

You might agree:
- To stop nagging the smoker about quitting, despite disliking smoking.
- To accept the smoker's habit, which is not the same as approving it. (Acceptance reflects an unconditional commitment to the smoker, as well as an understanding that the sole decision to smoke or quit lies solely with the person who smokes.)

And God's peace, which is so great we cannot understand it, will keep your hearts and minds in Christ Jesus.

Philippians 4: 7, The Answer

COPING, AS A NONSMOKER

There are some steps that nonsmoking family members, friends and co-workers can take to improve the quality of their own lives and their interactions with smokers:

1.) Stop making excuses for the smoker. Everyone has stress and problems, including nonsmokers. Smoking increases a smoker's pulse rate and blood pressure, thus adding to a person's stress, not reducing it as some smokers may think.

2.) Stop making it easy for a smoker to smoke. Do not give the smoker permission to smoke inside your house or car. Do not provide ashtrays or matches to smokers.

3.) When a smoker apologizes for smoking, accept the apology and stop there. Do not say, "Oh, we all have some little bad habit."

4.) Allow a smoker to experience the inconvenience and natural consequences of his or her smoking habit. Don't be rude; just don't accommodate the smoking habit. All of the cumulative negative aspects of smoking may motivate the smoker to quit.

5.) If the smoker is a mate, member of the immediate family or close friend, consider sharing specific concerns and issues with the smoker, without being hostile, self-righteous or overly dramatic.

6.) Enlisting the support of the smoker's health care providers. Studies have shown that even the briefest encouragement from a physician or dentist can motivate a smoker to quit.

7.) Giving the smoker encouragement and support if an effort is made to quit. Also, give the smoker space. Do not attempt to control or micromanage the quitting process.

Remember that the Lord your God is the only God and that He is faithful. He will keep His covenant and show His constant love to a thousand generations of those who love Him and obey His commands.

Deuteronomy 7: 9, The Good News Bible

ISSUES NONSMOKERS MAY
HAVE NOT CONSIDERED

❖❖❖

These comments are directed to nonsmokers who have a long-term and positive commitment to a smoker:

You may think that your "dyed-in-the-wool" smoker never thinks about quitting. You are probably wrong. In fact, many chronic, heavy smokers wish EVERY SINGLE DAY that they could stop smoking. But, rarely if ever will this category of smoker share thoughts about quitting with you.

Another possibility is that the smoker talks about quitting, yet refuses to set a quit day. This smoker is not serious about quitting. This smoker is playing games. "One of these days" is not one of the seven days of the week. Similarly, if a smoker says, "I'd like to quit BUT, ..." what the smoker really means is, "I have no intention of quitting, at least not now."

Quitting is probably a "hot button" issue for you and the smoker. I would like to help you better understand the resistance and anger a smoker may feel and exhibit when you talk about your desire for a smoker to quit.

Is it possible that you have unwisely and unfairly used the smoker's fears or intimate information to nag, threaten or humiliate? Have you repeatedly reminded the smoker of his or her past promises to quit?

Despite any strong negative feelings you may have about smoking, it is my opinion that nonsmokers do not have the authority to:
Judge smokers,
Tell smokers that they are stupid or foolish,
Seek retribution from smokers. (I.e., you "owe" me for all the aggravation you have caused me.)

I am sharing my opinions with you so that you (a nonsmoker) can better understand smoking and quitting issues. This does not mean that you should endorse anyone's smoking habit. Rather, I suggest that you use this information to communicate your unconditional love and encouragement for the smoker, regardless of whether the smoker chooses to smoke or to quit.

The Lord is near to those who are discouraged; he saves those who have lost all hope.

Psalm 34: 18, The Good News Bible

WHAT A NONSMOKER CAN DO TO BE SUPPORTIVE OF A SMOKER WHO CHOOSES TO QUIT

❖

Addiction of any kind is a family problem. The average smoker has at least seven people who markedly influence them and vice versa, including mate, children, parents, siblings, friends, co-workers and employer.

Research has shown that smokers who have the active support of family and friends have a higher level of success than do those who isolate and quit on their own.

Nonsmokers receive as many benefits from giving support, as does the smoker by receiving it. Consider giving the person who smokes space if/when:

❖ A decision is made to quit.
❖ Privacy is requested.
❖ A smoker tells you that he or she want to get through the quitting process without your help.

Respect the smoker's choices and resist telling him or her how you may have gotten through a similar problem. Also resist the temptation to share how you (or someone you know) stopped smoking. Smokers tend to be sensitive about receiving advice about quitting.

Do not be surprised if the smoker exhibits unusual behavior during the quitting process. It may feel like you are in the presence of a two-year-old who is having frequent temper tantrums or a moody teenager.

And for those who ask, "How long will the smoker's unusual behavior last?" Great question. There is no definitive answer; it varies for each smoker. Time is the best healer, tempered with lots of patience and love.

Trust in the Lord with all your heart, and do not rely on your own insight.

Proverbs 3: 5, Revised Standard Version

SUGGESTIONS FOR HEALTH CARE PROFESSIONALS

Physicians and dentists often underestimate the influence that they have with their patients who smoke or use nicotine products. The June 26, 2003 issue of *The New England Journal of Medicine* estimates that only twelve percent of smokers are advised by their physicians to quit.

A powerful motivation for a smoker to quit is hearing a physician or dentist say, "You need to stop smoking NOW. There are indications that cigarettes are damaging your _____. If you quit now, there is a good possibility that (list the probable health benefits that could occur), if you immediately quit smoking/chewing."

Health care professionals are advised to:
- Ask about and record the smoking status of every patient;
- Offer specific and current smoking cessation information to every smoker, during every office visit;
- Explain nicotine replacement products, as well as Wellbutrin, Zyban or comparable prescription medication to address depression, (if appropriate) to tobacco users, even if these products are not covered by the patient's insurance benefits.

Few smokers go to their doctors with questions or request advice about smoking, but patients may mention depression, anxiety or fatigue, which may be directly related to the patient's smoking habit.

In my opinion, the single biggest mistake health care professionals make in dealing with smokers is underestimating the complexity of the nicotine addiction. Negative comments such as the ones listed below should absolutely be avoided:
- If you don't want to smoke, just throw your cigarettes away.
- If you really want to quit, you'll just do it.
- I've known smokers who quit and never thought about cigarettes again. Quitting is no big thing.
- You're being so silly.
- You're such a baby.

Wanting to quit and knowing how to quit are two different things. A genuinely concerned professional should congratulate a smoker for being interested in quitting and should offer follow-up care and support.

Answer me, O Lord, for thy steadfast love is good; according to thy abundant mercy, turn to me. Hide not thy face from thy servant; for I am in distress, make haste to answer me.

Psalm 69: 16-17, Revised Standard Version

ACTIVITY: HOW I CAN SUPPORT MY SMOKER

It is not easy for me to remain quiet about issues that are of great importance to me. Maybe you feel that way toward the smoker in your life.

When someone you love is behaving or misbehaving in a way that threatens his or her health and well-being, as well as perhaps yours or others, what are the best actions to take?

Give the smoker your assurance that:

- Your love is unconditional.
- After having learned more about smoking, you can now better understand the difficulties of quitting.
- You will work to be less judgmental of the smoker, regardless of his or her decision about whether to quit or not.
- You will strive to improve your communication with the smoker, attempting to be more sensitive and honest.

There is no one complete or appropriate list that would address every smoker in every situation. But, I would think that most smokers would appreciate your sensitivity to them, and that the changes in your attitude and actions may open the door to better communication and positive results for both of you.

In my distress, I cry to the Lord, that he may answer me.

Psalm 120: 1, Revised Standard Version

ACTIVITY: IF MY SMOKER SHOULD EVER THINK ABOUT QUITTING

What action should you take if your smoker talks seriously about quitting?

I respond better to praise and the promise of a future reward than I do to skepticism or the threat of punishment for noncompliance. How about you?

Rather than offering a general promise of support to a smoker, think about what specific rewards or incentives you might suggest to a smoker if he or she quits?

Might any of these ideas be appropriate for you to offer your smoker?

During the first month after you quit, I will:

- Make coffee (or tea) for you every (morning, evening, weekend).
- Tell you three times a day (in person, by e-mail or phone) how proud I am of you.
- Have the inside of your car (or truck) detailed.

On your third month anniversary of not smoking, I would:

Babysit your child (or pet) so that _____.
Cook _____ or take you out to eat at _____ restaurant.

After six months of your not smoking, I would:
_____.

Be creative, generous and loving as you write your own list.

Now to Him who is able to keep you from stumbling, and to present you faultless before the presence of His glory with exceeding joy, to God our Savior, who alone is wise, by glory and majesty, dominion and power, both now and forever.

Jude 24-25, New King James Version

EPILOGUE

My hope for each smoker who reads this book is that you choose to quit. I want you to enjoy improved health, increased vitality, higher self-confidence and a more satisfying life as a nonsmoker.

In addition I pray that your Christian faith will be strengthened through the connections you made with God and other Christian-related resources during your stop smoking process.

I have found that when I put my life in God's hands, wonderful, exciting and fulfilling things happen that far exceed my fondest expectations. While God's blueprint is different for each of us, embrace God, who alone has the answers and peace you are seeking.

May you have a blessed and healthy life.

Judy Murphy Simpson

ABOUT THE AUTHOR

For more than fifteen years Judy Murphy Simpson has taught stop smoking classes and given seminars for thousands of health care professionals across the country.

She draws from her degrees in education and counseling, as well as from her personal history as a heavy smoker for twenty years.

Judy worked in various hospital and health care management positions. As a corporate marketing director, she wrote and presented in-service training programs and served as a smoking cessation consultant and staff trainer for two major health maintenance organizations.

She has also written and taught a Christian-based smoking cessation program: The Christian Connection. The scripted program and accompanying staff resource guidebook are available for purchase by individuals, church groups or organizations.

Judy and her husband, Gordon (Cork) Platts, live in southern California.

If you have comments about the book, would like to receive notification of other publications by this author or if you are interested in scheduling Judy Simpson as a speaker for your group, please e-mail her at judy1simpson@aol.com.

RESOURCE SECTION

TABLE: CIGARETTE NICOTINE LEVELS

HELPFUL WEB SITES

BIBLE VERSES QUOTED

SUGGESTED READING LIST

TABLE: CIGARETTE NICOTINE LEVELS

❖

In the United States cigarette manufacturers are not required to include the cigarette's nicotine level on cigarette packages or cartons. To obtain specific information about nicotine levels of U. S. brands of cigarettes, call the Federal Trade Commission: (202) 326-2222.

There are well over one hundred different cigarettes on the market. Most brands offer a wide range of strength, size and packaging options:

Filter or non-filter
Size lengths (120, 100, king or regular)
Menthol or non-menthol
Hardpack or soft pack
Full-flavor, lite or ultra-lite

So that you can get a general idea of how much nicotine your cigarettes may contain, I include a short list of popular U. S. cigarette brands. Please note that the nicotine categories and the brand placements are arbitrary and inexact.

BRANDS CONTAINING VERY HIGH LEVELS OF NICOTINE (ABOVE 1.2 MILIGRAMS): Lucky Strike non-filters, Newport 100, Old Gold King, Philip Morris, Salem King

BRANDS CONTAINING HIGH LEVELS OF NICOTINE (.8 TO 1.1 MILIGRAMS): Benson & Hedges, Camel, Capri, Doral, Eve, Kent, Kool, Lucky Strike, Marlboro, Newport King, Tareyton King, Viceroy, Virginia Slims 100, Winstons

BRANDS CONTAINING MEDIUM LEVELS OF NICOTINE (.4 TO .7 MILIGRAMS): Camel Ultralite, Eve Ultralite, Kool Ultralite, Marlboro Ultralite, Merit, Parliament, Salem Ultralite, Sterling, True, Virginia Slims Ultralite, Winston Ultralite

BRANDS CONTAINING LOW LEVELS OF NICOTINE (LESS THAN .3 MILIGRAMS): Barclay, Carlton, Next, Now

HELPFUL WEB SITES

❖

American Cancer Society: www.cancer.org (for local stop smoking information)

American Lung Association: www.lungusa.org/tobacco

Centers for Disease Control and Prevention: www.ccdc.gov/tobacco/how2quit.htm

National Cancer Institute: www.smokefree.gov

For chewers and dippers: www.cdc.gov/tobacco/how2quit.htm

QuitNet to sign up for a stop smoking buddy: www.quitnet.com

Tobacco Cessation Guideline: www.surgeongeneral.gov/tobacco/

BIBLE VERSES QUOTED

OLD TESTAMENT	
Genesis	35: 2
Deuteronomy	4: 23-24
	7: 9
	29: 18-19
	30: 9
	32: 2-3
Joshua	10: 6
	24: 23
I Samuel	15: 22-23
	17: 37
2 Samuel	22: 2-4
I Kings	10: 9
I Chronicles	22: 19
Nehemiah	4: 10
Job	15: 31
Psalm	2: 4
	25: 7
	27: 1
	30: 2
	34: 18
	46: 1-3
	61: 1-4

	64: 1
	69: 1-2
	69: 16-17
	81: 9
	109: 26-28
	118: 24
	120: 1
	121: 1-2
Proverbs	3: 5
	13: 20
	15: 32
	16: 3
	16: 32
	29: 11
Ecclesiastes	1: 8-9
	3: 1
	7: 8
Song of Solomon	4: 1
Isaiah	12: 1
	26: 4
	28: 16
	30: 21
	40: 31
	41: 4
	41: 10
	43: 1-3
	44: 2
	44: 6
	50: 7
	51: 1

Jeremiah	3: 22
	6: 16
	7: 23
	7: 24
	17: 7
	17: 14
	33: 3
Ezekiel	12: 1-2
Nahum	2: 1
Habakkuk	3: 17-19
Haggai	1: 5
Malachi	3: 6
NEW TESTAMENT	
Matthew	7: 7-8
	19: 26
	24: 13
	28: 20
Mark	6:; 31
	11: 23
Luke	1: 37
	9: 62
John	8: 12
	8: 31-32

	14: 27
Acts	Chapter 1
Romans	8: 81
	12: 2
	13: 9
	15: 13
I Corinthians	3: 8
	6: 19-20
	15: 33
	15: 34
2 Corinthians	6: 14 -15
	12: 9
Galatians	5: 16
	6: 4-5
	6: 9
Ephesians	6: 16
Philippians	3: 12
	3: 13-14
	4: 7
	4: 9
I Thessalonians	5: 3-4
	5: 17
I Timothy	4: 8
2 Timothy	1: 7
	2: 22

Hebrews	12: 1-2
	6: 11-12
	12: 12-13
James	1: 5
	1: 12
	1: 14
	2: 8
	4: 8
I Peter	2: 9
	4: 12-13
	5: 10-11
I John	1: 8-9
2 John	8
Jude	24 – 25
Revelations	14: 12

SUGGESTED READING LIST

❖

Beattie, Melody, *The Language of Letting Go*, Harper Collins Publishers, New York, 1990

Buscagglia, Ph.D., Leo, *Living, Loving and Learning*, Fawcett Columbine Book, New York, 1982

Dayton, Ph.D., Tian, *Forgiving and Moving On*, Health Communications, Inc., Deerfield FL, 1992

Donihue, Anita Corrine, *When I'm on My Knees*, Barbour & Company, Inc., Uhrichsville OH, 1973

Fox, Emmet, *The Sermon on the Mount*, Harper San Francisco, 1934

Graham, Billy, *The Inspirational Writings – Peace with God, The Secret of Happiness, Answers to Life's Problems*, Inspirational Press, New York, 1995

Larsen, Earnie and Hegarty, Carol Larsen, *Days of Healing Days of Joy*, Hazeldon Foundation, 1987

Link, Mark, *Jesus Beyond 2000*, Thomas More, Allen TX, 1997

Moody, D. L., *365 Days a Year with D. L. Moody*, Fleming H. Revell, Grand Rapids MI, 1995

Peale, Norman Vincent, *The Positive Power of Jesus Christ*, Foundation for Christian Living, Pawling NY, 1980

Quezada, Adolfo, *Loving Yourself for God's Sake*, Resurrection Press, Ltd., Williston Park, NY, 1997

Pitino, Rick, *Success Is a Choice*, Broadway Books, New York, 1997

Rupp, Joyce, *The Cup of Our Life*, Ave Maria Press, Notre Dame IN, 1997

Rupp, Joyce, *Inviting God In*, Ave Maria Press, Notre Dame IN, 2001

Rupp, Joyce, *May I Have This Dance?* Ave Maria Press, Notre Dame IN, 1992

Rupp, Joyce, *Your Sorrow Is My Sorrow,* Crossroad Publishing Co., New York, 1999

Schaef, Anne Wilson, *Meditations for Women Who Do Too Much,* Harper San Francisco, 1990

Stanley, Charles F., *The Power of the Cross,* Thomas Nelson Publishers, Nashville TN, 1998

Stanley, Charles F., *The Savior's Touch,* Zondervan Publishing House, Grand Rapids MI, 1996

Stanley, Charles F., The Source of My Strength, Thomas Nelson Publishers, Nashville TN, 1994

Swindoll, Charles R., *Growing Strong in the Seasons of Life,* Multnomah, Portland OR, 1983

Thoele, Sue Patton, *Freedoms after 50,* Conari Press, Berkeley CA, 1998

Thoele, Sue Patton, *The Courage to Be Yourself,* MJF Books, New York, 1988

Vanzant, Iyanla, *In the Meantime,* Simon & Schuster, New York, 1998

Vanzant, Iyanla, *Until Today,* Simon & Schuster, New York, 2000

Vanzant, Iyanla, *The Value in the Valley,* Simon & Schuster, New York, 1995

Lightning Source UK Ltd.
Milton Keynes UK
UKHW011826090920
369608UK00001B/60